JESUS, *the* MAN WHO LOVED WOMEN

To Noreen —

His love
heals all!

Love —

Jo

BRUCE MARCHIANO

JESUS, *the* MAN WHO LOVED WOMEN

He Treasures, Esteems, *and* Delights in You

HOWARD BOOKS
A DIVISION OF SIMON & SCHUSTER
New York   London   Toronto   Sydney

Our purpose at Howard Books is to:

- *Increase faith* in the hearts of growing Christians
- *Inspire holiness* in the lives of believers
- *Instill hope* in the hearts of struggling people everywhere

Because He's coming again!

Published by Howard Books, a division of Simon & Schuster, Inc.
1230 Avenue of the Americas, New York, NY 10020
HOWARD www.howardpublishing.com
BOOKS

Jesus, the Man Who Loved Women © 2008 Bruce Marchiano

Library of Congress Cataloging-in-Publication Data

Marchiano, Bruce.
   Jesus, the man who loved women : He treasures, esteems, and delights in you / Bruce Marchiano.
      p. cm.
   ISBN–13: 978-1-4165-4397-8 (trade paper)
   ISBN–10:   1-4165-4397-X
   1. Women in the Bible. 2. Christian women—Religious life. I. Title.

BS2445.M27   2008
226'.0922082—dc22   2008005016

10 9 8 7 6 5 4

Manufactured in the United States of America

For information regarding special discounts for bulk purchases, please contact: Simon & Schuster Special Sales at 1-800-456-6798 or business @simonandschuster.com.

Interior design by Jaime Putorti

Unless otherwise noted, all Scripture quotations are from *The Holy Bible, New International Version®* Copyright © 1973, 1978, 1984 by International Bible Society. Used by permission of Zondervan. All rights reserved. Scripture quotations marked (NLT) are taken from the *Holy Bible, New Living Translation,* copyright © 1996. Used by permission of Tyndale House Publishers, Inc., Wheaton, Illinois 60189. All rights reserved. Italics in Scripture quotations were added by the author for emphasis.

To my father—

I miss you, Pop

CONTENTS

vii

Flowers appear on the earth; the season of singing has come, the cooing of doves is heard in our land.

—Song of Songs 2:12

Imagine a Man

One of my favorite phrases of all time is from the musical stage play *Man of La Mancha*. I will never forget hearing it for the very first time when, at the age of eighteen, I went to see a local production. I was a college student majoring in performing arts at California State University–Fullerton. I had my eyes firmly set on an acting career, and to say that *Man of La Mancha* was one of my foremost inspirations woould be a huge understatement.

I remember buying the soundtrack from the original Broadway musical starring the now-deceased Richard Kiley in the role of Don Quixote. In those days the music was on an LP, and I played that LP until the grooves were worn flat. I spent whole afternoons acting out the entire production in my living room, singing every song, playing every role, over and over, day after day. I was the hero, Don Quixote. I was his faithful squire, Sancho. I was the Padre, or the Innkeeper, and I would act out complete scenes, even dialoguing back and forth between the characters.

All these years later, I can still remember most every line from most every song. There's the timeless and most well known, "The Impossible Dream." There's the love song of love songs, "Dulcinea"; the triumphant "I, Don Quixote"; the hilarious "I Really Like Him"; and on and on. Truly, to this day I could do the entire musical in a one-man show (now wouldn't that be a comedy!).

If perchance you aren't familiar with *Man of La Mancha*, it's a story that is as simple as it is profound. It's a play within a play that takes place in centuries-ago Spain—an era during which Spain and much of Europe was mired in terrible darkness and oppression. Dictatorship, disease, and poverty reigned across the continent, and it was "survival of the fittest." The order of the day was dog-eat-dog, and every man was for himself.

The play begins when a playwright and idealist named Miguel de Cervantes is thrown into an Inquisition dungeon packed with the most vile and vicious criminals and cutthroats. He has with him a trunk that contains an unfinished manuscript as well as costumes, stage makeup, etc. The manuscript is the story of Don Quixote, a broken-down old man who fancies himself a knight from the mythical La Mancha. The baddies in the dungeon descend upon Cervantes, anxious to get their hands on everything he has.

Cervantes clings to the manuscript, even to the point that his life is at risk. He pleads to keep all that is in his beloved trunk—to him, the story represents goodness, righteousness, virtue, and hope. In desperation he proposes that he stage the story of Don Quixote for them right there in the dungeon and says that if they are not moved by its values, they can have their way. All agree, and the drama begins.

This is where that favorite phrase comes in. The criminals settle down, the lights dim, and Cervantes slowly opens the trunk as if it contains the most fragile and precious of treasures. He lays out his Don Quixote makeup, most ceremoniously a moustache and pointy white beard. He dips his fingers into a jar of glue. He spreads it around his mouth and across his chin. Then ever so slowly, almost religiously, he lifts the beard to his face and presses it into position. As he does so, he breathes these words in sacred awe: "Imagine a man." As he speaks the words, Don Quixote de La Mancha is born.

As Cervantes' play unfolds, we discover that Don Quixote is an old man who is so besieged by the ugliness and horror of the real world that he has retreated into an imaginary fairy-tale world. In his mind's eye, he is in the era of noble knights, damsels in distress, virtuous kings, and glimmering castles. He himself is a knight whose mission is to uphold chivalry, battle all evil, and right all that is wrong.

He comes upon a windmill and perceives it to be a dragon. He attacks it with hilarious profundity. He enters a ramshackle inn that is actually a haven for highwaymen and prostitutes. But in Don Quixote's eyes, the innkeeper is a lord and the inn is his manor. A traveling barber's shaving basin is the glorious Golden Helmet of Mambrino.

More wonderful than anything else in Don Quixote's make-believe world of nobility, beauty, cause, and right, there is a woman—Aldonza. In reality Aldonza is a brazen, harder-than-cement (forgive me for using the specific language of the play) "whore." At the inn, she serves men their drinks and then serves them herself. She proudly boasts, "All you need do is cross my palm with a coin"; and that's exactly how it goes, all day long, every long day—your room or my room, the barn or the bushes.

Aldonza is a woman who has long ago forgotten womanhood. She has never known virtue, dignity, care, or respect. She is like an old piece of leather both inside and out, and her bottom line is cold, hard cash.

When Don Quixote enters the inn, Aldonza sees only a new prospect. She approaches him with a jug of spirits. She bends low and makes sure that her all is in view. She throws her leg on the chair and raises her skirt, making sure that even more is in view.

But Aldonza has never met a man like Don Quixote—a man who sees none of what Aldonza has become at the hands of a cruel world. When he lifts his eyes to meet hers, instead of laughing, he gasps. Overcome to have looked upon such breathtaking beauty, he drops to his knee and lowers his face. His lips quiver in awe as they carefully whisper, "My lady . . ."

You see, in Don Quixote's eyes there is no Aldonza. In his eyes the woman who stands before him baring her wares is anything but a whore. She is the picture of virtue, exquisite in beauty and grace. She is a human rose, a living seascape, the fullness of all that makes life worth living. She is "the Lady Dulcinea," and he is her devoted knight, sworn to honor and protect her, to shield her from all evil, to give his life should it be so required.

Don Quixote sees none of the grime that stains Aldonza's cheeks or the dread lines that inscribe hardship across her brow. The burlap rags that almost clothe her body are as silk and velvet in his eyes, and her shameless swagger is the glissade of graciousness. When this "imagine a man" looks upon Aldonza the whore, he sees only who Aldonza *really* is beneath all that her whore-ific history has made of her. All that this man sees is Dulcinea.

In the pages that follow, you and I are going to meet a number of women. These women are not fictional like Aldonza; they are very real women who lived very real lives two thousand years ago. It knocks the wind out of me to write the words, but some of the women we'll meet lived lives very much like

Aldonza's. Some of them lived very much the opposite. Some of them, may I humbly whisper, may have lived lives similar to your own.

You see, it's a fascinating and unarguable reality: times may have changed. Technology may have developed. Surface considerations may differ from nation to nation, culture to culture, and generation to generation. But deep beneath it all, transcending it all, there is one thing that stays eternally the same—the human heart. That which the heart desires and longs for, that which warms and secures and cradles it in peace—these are still the same.

Come with me and meet these precious women. Let us peek inside their hearts and glimpse their hopes and passions. Let us cry with them, laugh with them, face their challenges, feel the weight of their disappointments, and experience the joy of their fulfillments. These precious women are everywoman. And who knows? One or two of them may even be you.

I would also invite you to "imagine a man." This man was also very real, having lived two thousand years ago just as these women we will soon meet. Like them, he laughed and cried. He toiled and tried and planned and purposed. He laid down his head at the end of every long, hard day and rested in the cool of every long, hard night.

The human condition that met this man's eyes was bleak at best. Just like Don Quixote's Spain, everywhere he looked there was oppression and hard times. The rich were stealing from the poor, and the poor were stealing from each other. The religious were mostly pomp and splendor, and the nonreligious were . . . well . . . at least they weren't pretending.

Admittedly, the people of Israel—the land in which both he and these women lived—had a remarkable tenacity, and after generations of persecution, they had learned to squeeze goodness from life's dregs. Still, there was no denying the hardship, and so they cried out to the living God for his long-promised Messiah who, like Don Quixote, would march into their midst on a mission to right all that was wrong. He would be a savior, and his character would be such that he would willingly, as the lyrics of "The Impossible Dream" so eloquently proclaim, "march into hell for a heavenly cause."

This man was that Messiah, and the day would surely come when he would fulfill his march into the worst of hell. But that's not what this book is about. This book is not about his deeds in divinity. This book is about him as a man. It's about his character and quality, most specifically in relationship and interaction with those very women.

You see, between his days of youth and that day of hell, this man would cross paths with every one of them. They would look into his eyes. They would lean on the tenor of his voice. They would glimpse his heart—some over long periods of friendship and others in moments of passing. Some would only know him from across a courtyard, and others would get close enough to experience his touch. But they would all experience his person.

Like Aldonza with Don Quixote, they would all see themselves through the eyes of his heart.

We all know who this man is by now, and so let us consider what a woman would have experienced two thousand years ago in the presence of Jesus. What would a woman have learned in a moment of human interaction with this man who was God? What would she have seen in his eyes or heard in the lilt of his voice? As he placed his hand upon her shoulder, how would that hand have felt to her? What message would it have whispered into her heart? What pureness of care would have washed her every "Aldonza" away?

This is what we will explore in the pages that follow. We'll meet these precious women in the gospel stories of Matthew, Mark, Luke, and John. There, we'll also meet Jesus afresh and anew. We'll use our imaginations to peek into the possibilities and probabilities of their emotions and circumstances. We'll eavesdrop as they stand eye to eye. We'll listen to their laughter, share their tears, and taste of those two-thousand-year-old feelings that are still a part of every woman's heart today.

Jesus Christ is the same yesterday
and today and forever.
—*Hebrews 13:8*

Come to me [oh precious woman], . . .
and I will give you rest. . . . I am gentle
and humble in heart,
and you will find rest for your soul.
—Matthew 11:28–29

In the climatic scene of *Man of La Mancha*, Don Quixote is lying on his deathbed. A character called the "Knight of the Mirrors" has forced him to face who he really is. The encounter shatters his "impossible dream" of a world that can be won over by gallantry and goodness. The dream was his life, and so with the destruction of that dream, his life ebbs away.

Aldonza kneels at Quixote's side. Deeply affected by his blindness to her dirt and having never before tasted untainted love, she pleads with him to live. She begs him to reclaim the dream and, thereby, restore the dream that has claimed her own heart. Aldonza desperately sings to him the same love song he had sung to her—and Quixote stirs. The light returns to his eyes as he wonders aloud, "Maybe it wasn't only a dream." Aldonza seizes the moment with, "You told me about a dream . . ." and Quixote stirs even more. Through tears of hope, she repeats the timeless virtues captured in "The Impossible Dream," and it works! Quixote leaps from his bed, as new life explodes in his heart.

What happens next has always been beyond breathtaking to me, even way back when I was a clumsy eighteen-year-old sitting in the cheap seats with my mouth hanging open. Having just risen from near death, Quixote turns to Aldonza and says words so remarkable that, again, I remember them to this day. He says, "This is not right, my lady, that you would be on your knees to me."

There is no thought for himself. There is only, "My lady." There is only, "You are so precious." There is only Dulcinea.

Moments later, much weakened, Quixote falls in death. The innkeeper turns to Aldonza and beckons her to return to her work—to return to her life as it was. He says, "Come, let's go, Aldonza." But she doesn't follow. Instead, she straightens and replies, "My name is Dulcinea."

And Jesus, the Son of the living God—he who conceived and birthed you and held you in his heart before you ever came to be—whispers to you, *Your name, oh precious woman, is Dulcinea.*

His banner over me is love.
—*Song of Songs 2:4*

Come away, precious woman, come away. Come away with Jesus!

JESUS.

You are the most excellent of men
and your lips have been anointed with grace,
since God has blessed you forever.

—Psalm 45:2

"Before Abraham Was Born, I Am!"

*I*t was many years ago that I postured myself to discover who Jesus *really* was as a man two thousand years ago. If I may share the abridged version of that story, I'd been raised in a Christian home and educated in Christian schools. All through my twenties I attended church regularly and had a serious belief in God. At thirty, I was finally born again and lived excitedly in a new relationship with Jesus. My life became joyously filled with Bible studies, brotherhood, and heartfelt worship. Then one day, in the middle of it all, I was struck with the realization that in spite of all I'd learned and embraced in faith and belief, I had never taken the time to get to know *him*.

Oh yes, I knew all about him. I knew every gospel story and every gospel character. I could tell you why Jesus stepped out of heaven and why he allowed us to nail him to that tree. I could quote John 3:16 and many scriptures more. I was saved and well on my way to a glorious eternity in the wonder of his presence. I just didn't know him—as a man in his personhood, character, and heart. As much as I knew Jesus in the Christianese sense of the word, I had no idea who he really was.

I dare to guess I'm not the only one who can tell that story. Sometimes even in the middle of our most sincere and godly intentions we can miss the forest through the trees. Sometimes one's Christianity can become more about other things than about Jesus. Granted, they may be wonderful and valuable—but just not *him*.

We can also fall victim to that age-old adage: familiarity breeds contempt. Sadly, Jesus is probably the ultimate example of its heartbreaking truth. Especially in today's Christian world, where there always seems to be something new and upcoming, that which is fundamental can be so easily overlooked. That which is simple ceases to excite. Regardless of importance or vitalness, much like breathing, that which costs nothing (as in Jesus who comes freely) can be so easily taken for granted.

So right there in the middle of our highest hallelujahs he stands, longing to be desired and pursued, longing to be what excites us most of all. With outreached arms and perhaps a mist of tears softening the fire in his eyes, he stands amidst all the bells and whistles that compete for our Christian attention, longing to be the obsession of our hearts.

And so there came the day when I laid everything aside and set my heart on knowing Jesus. I opened up the "grand ol' Book" and chased the familiarity from its pages. I immersed myself in the streets of ancient Israel; I pressed myself into their living, breathing, *human* situations.

You will seek me and find me when
you seek me with all your heart.
—*Jeremiah 29:13*

The Gospels ceased to be so much about "the original Greek"—as valuable as that understanding is—and became more about people. They became about men and women who were no different from you or me, who were doing their best to negotiate life in a world that was as challenging then as ours is today.

The gospel stories became about their hearts and minds and hopes and dreams, about their failures and victories, their joys and tragedies. The stories became about their search for God, even as he stood humanly manifest before them.

But high and above those layers, the Gospels became about what they are most supposed to be about—*Jesus.* Oh most wondrous Jesus! They became about the Son of the living God who loved his children so much that he relinquished every divine privilege to walk and live among them. They became about the Son of the living God who "made himself nothing" for you and me.

Who, being in very nature God,
did not consider equality with God something to be grasped,
but made himself nothing,
taking the very nature of a servant,
being made in human likeness.
And being found in appearance as a man,
he humbled himself
and became obedient to death—
even death on a cross!

—Philippians 2:6–8

So where do we begin our quest to know the man Jesus? How do we discover his heart and person? It has been said that the heart of a man is revealed in his actions. That being true, we begin in the land of Israel a long time ago. We begin with Jesus.

He grew up before him like a tender shoot,
and like a root out of dry ground.
He had no beauty or majesty to attract us to him,
nothing in his appearance that we should desire him.

—Isaiah 53:2

Two thousand years ago Jesus was a very real man, albeit more "real" than any man who walked the earth before or after him. His appearance was nothing like the paintings, films, and lyrical descriptions that are so much a part of our religious tradition and culture. He was not necessarily taller, for example, than everyone around him—as he is so often portrayed. His clothes were not all gleaming white while everyone else's were earthen brown.

There was nothing in his visage or stance that carried even a hint of heavenly splendor. As the scripture above makes clear, to the human eye there was absolutely nothing about him that would have set him apart from anyone else of his day. Aside from his divinity and glory of mission, he was "just another working man" making his living by the sweat of his brow—a carpenter by trade who earned his keep with the strength in his hands and the tools his father taught him to use. It's how he spent the majority of his life—sawing wood, hammering nails, sanding, planing, carving, and molding.

Picture his arms, thick and sinewy, dark and tanned, stained with sawdust and sweat. Picture the soil embedded beneath his fingernails and seated deep in the wrinkles of his knuckles. Picture the sun-baked furrows that stretch across the breadth of his most holy brow; the calluses, scrapes, bruises, and scars. Picture the barrel of his chest and the girth of his trunk, not like a weightlifter or athlete of today but like a man who works. And *works*.

Using our imaginations, picture Jesus at the end of a twelve-hour workday. His robes are soiled from top to bottom with pine tar, wood sap, and grit. Hand-me-downs from his father—whose laughter Jesus deeply misses since that day he passed on—are now so worn and threadbare. Patched and repatched, they are oh so close to his heart.

There's a rag knotted around his forearm where earlier his homemade saw had snapped under the pressure of too much torque and torn into his flesh. He had no time to stop and tend the wound. There was too much to be done and too many deadlines breathing down his neck. So the blood was quickly wiped against the other sleeve, and the closest rag became first aid. Then it was back to work.

Now the sun has gone, and night has taken over. His eyes are fatigued, and the candles he'd planted about his workbench are no longer doing the trick. He's making more mistakes, and progress has slowed. And so Jesus sets his tools down. He stops and takes a long, deep breath. He rakes the sawdust from the whiskers of his beard. Finally, Jesus closes the door on another long, hard day.

He walks to the well and draws an urn of deep spring water. He spills its icy cold over his face and scrubs himself alert. He lifts his head and shakes back his mane. He runs his hands through its thickness with fingers that are sore from the beating they took today and so many other days.

He sits quietly, resting in the cool night air. His gaze turns upward toward the moonlit sky as he drags a rag across his face, wiping it clean of the day's toil. It's quiet, so quiet. In the stillness of his heart, Jesus thanks his earthly father for passing on the skills by which he earns his daily bread, and he thanks his heavenly Father for the bread he ate that day.

That's how Jesus spent most of his life: *working*, no different from you or me.

The Word became flesh and made his dwelling among us.
—John 1:14

JESUS.

Jesus went to a town called Nain,
and his disciples and a large crowd went along with him.
As he approached the town gate,
a dead person was being carried out—
the only son of his mother, and she was a widow.
—Luke 7:11–12

I imagine it was a day like any other in ancient Galilee. I don't know what the weather was like; no one can say with certainty. But since gospel events tend to be presented in the warm glow of sunshine and beauty, let's imagine that it was a hard, cold wintry day—if only to be different . . .

No one in or around the bustling town of Nain could remember cold like this. Many fathers had moved their families there just because its weather was relatively mild. Now with an icy wind blasting off the snows that blanket Mount Hermon in the distance, families sit huddled around the fire, day after day, hoping the terrible chill will break.

Since Nain is a farming community, everyone is concerned. What will such cold do to the crops and orchards? Their fruit trees are generations old, and now they stand bitten by frost and struggling to endure. If Yahweh doesn't answer Nain's prayers very soon, all may be lost. What would they do in the coming year? How would they meet taxation's harsh levy? How would Nain survive?

The old widow considers none of these worries, however, as she sits by her son's much-too-still remains. With what little she had left, she'd purchased the linen and spices that now embrace his body. She'd bought the brier on which he so silently lies. Soon they will come, and the procession will begin. Soon he will be taken from her forever and buried outside Nain's gates.

He was her only son. She'd had such trouble conceiving, but the husband she'd buried just a few years ago had so gallantly stood by her. He did not leave her, as so many men would have. He simply said, "Let's keep trying, and let's keep praying." And Yahweh was faithful to hear their cries. A child was born, and what's more, it was a son who would carry on the family name.

There was such great rejoicing that day! They were both so concerned that something would be wrong with the baby, yet everything had come out right. Everything seemed right, anyway. The boy grew strong like any other boy. He thrived and excelled and made both Mom and Dad proud.

How were they to know that frailties lay hidden deep within his cell structure? How were they to know that one day those frailties would rise to the surface and overtake him?

So much pain, so many doctors, and so many prayers in desperation would follow. Then came the day when Dad died, leaving Mom with her son. Together the two of them continued to cry out to God and hold on to hope. Together they traveled far and farther and sought expert after expert; and it seemed that the weaker he got, the more hopeful they both became—the more confident they grew that God would intervene.

But now this woman sits alone—a mother alone with her son.

Never mind her fears of the future. Never mind the confusion of unanswered prayer. Never mind the anger at God and the frustration with doctors and the second-guessing of all that's gone before. She is a mother, and he is her son. And so she sits quietly in their final moments together.

Perhaps there are no more tears in her eyes. She has cried all she has . . . for now. Perhaps exhaustion has overtaken emotion, and so she just sits—still and alone. She looks to the window to see if anyone is yet coming to take him away. She waves off a fly that hovers over his chest. "I'm going to miss you, son," she whispers. It's all she can think to say. "I'm going to miss you so much."

Is that scenario how it really happened? Of course, we can't know. But we do know this: in the sea of her sorrow, this precious mother has no idea of the man she is about to meet. She has no idea that he is God in the flesh and that he has counted her every tear all these years. She has no idea that this man—whose name is Jesus and whose name means "God Saves"—is always the answer to every tear.

As friends and family come to carry her son away, she can't conceive of the quality of man that is this man. She can't begin to imagine that at the core of his manhood is deep understanding of her womanhood and even deeper compassion for her mother-hood. She has no idea that at the heart of his person is love—for her.

Who is this, robed in splendor, striding forward in the greatness of his strength? "It is I, speaking in righteousness, mighty to save."

—Isaiah 63:1

JESUS.

*As he approached the town gate, a dead person was being
carried out—the only son of his mother,
and she was a widow. And a large crowd from the town was
with her. When the Lord saw her,
his heart went out to her and he said, "Don't cry."*
—*Luke 7:12–13*

What facts do we know about what happened that Nain day?
We know this is the only gospel story that mentions the town
of Nain. We know that many scholars believe Jesus had been in
Capernaum just the day before. We know that Jesus traveled by
foot—and that Nain was *twenty-five miles away.*

Why would Jesus turn his course toward Nain and march that
great distance? How did he just happen to arrive at Nain's gate just
as this woman and her son were passing through?

Of course every move Jesus made was a purposeful fulfillment
of the Law and the Prophets. Every move was intended to proclaim,
I AM (Exodus 3:14). Every moment of his life and every decision
Jesus made was a perfect orchestration of his Father's perfect plan.

But sometimes in the singular focus on big-picture answers,
we can so easily bypass *him.* We can miss that in the midst of all
those wondrous realities stood a very real man—a man who made
choices and got hurt and loved and cared. A man who tasted fatigue and hunger, joy and disappointment. This man Jesus was
real.

So why did Jesus go to Nain that day? Notwithstanding all those big and important answers, he went to Nain because he "knows." In his divine understanding, he's heard this precious mother's every cry in the night and measured her every heartache throughout every day.

You see, Jesus knows a woman's fears and frustrations, hurt and fatigue. He knows how loss can cut through a woman's being and pierce her woman's heart. He understands that moment when a mother's son is no more. Jesus *knows*.

Why would Jesus walk twenty-five miles to get to Nain? As Luke writes, "When the Lord saw her, his heart went out to her." Yes, it was all in his heart. *She* was in his heart—his man heart, his God heart. The answers are always in his heart.

JESUS.

And he said, "Don't cry."
—*Luke 7:13*

As the Gospel of Luke records, those were the only two words Jesus spoke to this precious woman that day. They were words that were so human, so genuine—spoken only to her. We can only imagine Jesus' sure and gracious tone as the words so gently fell from his lips. We can only imagine the warmth and respect, the comfort and kindness, the intimacy and care. There the two of them stood, surrounded by so many, but in that moment, she was his entire world.

"Don't cry," he whispered. I picture a wash of tears misting over his own eyes in that moment. She had been through so much, this precious woman who filled the volume of his heart. And I can only imagine the words he didn't give voice to but spoke so clearly through his gaze and the humble restraint that was always his masculine way. Perhaps he reached one of his thick, calloused hands to cradle her cheek softly. Perhaps he even took her into the fold of his strong carpenter's arms and held her closely to his God-man chest.

I see and I know, his silence breathes into every corner of her bruised and broken heart. *I've come just for you. I've come to wipe every tear away.*

And that's exactly what Jesus did. "Young man, I say to you, get up! The dead man sat up and began to talk, and Jesus gave him back to his mother" (Luke 7:14–15). Oh, what a moment that must have been. What emotion must have rocketed through that mother's heart. For so long, all she'd known was weeping and disappointment, loss and ache. Now, all of that was nothing. It was as if it had never been. Grief was replaced with joy. Tears turned to laughter. Where there had only been aloneness, hopelessness, and meals in silence—now there was her precious son, alive again.

"He lives, he lives!" The cry must have echoed from Nain's city gate to every village in Galilee. "At the touch of Jesus, at the sound of his voice, the boy lives!"

JESUS.

Who was this man Jesus two thousand years ago? It has been said that a man's heart is revealed by his choices and his actions.

Jesus walked twenty-five miles. He gave a son back to his mother. He whispered, "Don't cry." The boy lives!

This is who the man Jesus was two thousand years ago. This is who he was that day for that precious woman who had cried so many tears—and this is who he is for you, oh precious woman, today.

Can you feel his rugged hand cradling your own cheek? Can you see the warmth, respect, and care—for you—that fills his eyes to overflowing? Can you feel his arms enfold you in a most holy embrace and hear his whisper in the quiet of your heart? . . .

I AM for you, my precious one. I AM the banner that stretches over your woman's heart. I come to bring light where darkness encroaches and to breathe grace and mercy where injury abounds. I come to arrest that which would rise against you and try to crush your loveliness of soul.

This world is broken, my precious one, and it so often breaks upon you. I have come that you might have life, instead. I have come that you might celebrate.

You abide so deep in my kingdom heart. I count your tears. I cry them with you. It is my wondrous pleasure to wipe them all away and turn your every mourning into joy.

No distance is too great for me to travel. No divide is too wide. No sacrifice is too costly. Indeed, I have given my life—for you.

I love you, my precious daughter. I love you.

JESUS.

He passed in front of Moses, proclaiming, "The LORD, the LORD, the compassionate and gracious God, slow to anger, abounding in love and faithfulness."

—Exodus 34:6

Filled with compassion, Jesus reached out his hand and touched the man. "I am willing," he said. "Be clean!"

—Mark 1:41

I love you.

JESUS.

A woman was there who had been

subject to bleeding for twelve years. . . .

When she heard about Jesus,

she came up behind him in the crowd

and touched his cloak, because she thought,

"If I just touch his clothes,

I will be healed."

—*Mark 5:25–28*

"Take Heart, Daughter"

She was a woman. She was bleeding. Twelve years. From her womb.

Through the centuries this woman's story has been told and retold. It stands as one of the most iconic stories in all the gospels. Jesus was moving through a crowd on his way to raise a little girl from the dead—the daughter of a synagogue ruler named Jairus—when he felt someone's "touch." He turned, and there stood this woman. She had pressed through the throng that surrounded Jesus, thinking, "If I only touch his cloak, I will be healed" (Matthew 9:21), and she was right. The bleeding stopped then and there.

Much has been made of the unique circumstances surrounding this woman and her miracle. There is the fact that it seemingly occurred without Jesus' specific intent. There are also his words, "I know that power has gone out from me" (Luke 8:46). Volumes of commentary have been written, and there's been so much debate, in attempts to determine exactly what that statement means.

More than any other aspect of this gospel encounter, it is this woman's determination and faith that has attracted the most attention. Jesus' words to her, "Your faith has healed you" (Matthew 9:22), comprise one of the most quoted scriptures among "faith teachers" in support of their doctrine. Of course those who would argue with them often use the very same words to claim their own positions.

But two thousand years ago, there was none of this discussion. Jesus' words had nothing to do with doctrine. He was not concerned with scriptural debate or interpretation of phrases. On that first-century day Jesus was simply a man who stood eye to eye with a woman—and she was simply a woman who stood face to face with the God who'd created her.

Through him all things were made;
without him nothing was made that has been made.
—*John 1:3*

You created my inmost being;
you knit me together in my mother's womb.
—*Psalm 139:13*

JESUS.

What must that have been like for Jesus when he turned to look into that precious woman's eyes that day? From the beginning of time, she lay deep in his divine heart. His desire for her to be was the very force that gave her life. He'd planned her from head to toe, inside and out, and then finally there came that split second that was her perfect beginning.

With all the anticipation of the universe stretched across his face in a heavenly smile, he breathed the breath of life into her mother's womb. He whispered the words he'd longed to whisper and couldn't wait one more second to whisper: *Live, my precious one. I love you so much. Live!*

In my imagination I picture all the angels that are gathered about his throne leaping to their feet in that most wondrous moment. After all, is it not life that is heaven's greatest passion? Is it not the execution of God's most excellent will that is all of creation's greatest joy?

I imagine a thunder of celebration rising from their multitudes. I hear their bliss-filled shout bounce and echo off eternity's walls. "Hosanna in the highest," they cry. "Hosanna in the highest! The one he loves—the one he desires—she lives!"

And so Jesus rolls up his divine sleeves to begin the blessed business of crafting this woman who is already so precious to him. He shapes her frame and shades her skin. He molds her mind and measures her stature. He sculpts the contour of her face, the almonds of her eyes, and the graceful stretch of her limbs. Long before she has ever spoken a word, he has held her voice in his heart, and so he ever-so-gently tunes its timbre. Cell by cell, tenderness by tenderness, and with care beyond care, in creation he quite simply *loves her.*

Yes, as Jesus stood there looking into this woman's eyes that day, he saw eyes that he himself had chosen for her, and in his heart he had already looked into them many times. He had planned this very moment, in fact, and the warmth that rose in him when she lifted her countenance finally to meet his was nothing new or novel. He'd felt that warmth for her long before she was even born. He'd felt it since that very first moment when he'd first conceived her deep in his heart.

My frame was not hidden from you
when I was made in the secret place.
When I was woven together in the depths of the earth,
your eyes saw my unformed body.
All the days ordained for me
were written in your book
before one of them came to be.
—Psalm 139:15–16

JESUS.

And what of this woman two thousand years ago? Who was this woman? What would twelve years of bleeding do to such a woman?

I think of that very first day and that very first drop that whispered a cry for attention. My guess is that the cry went largely ignored. I imagine that it got little more than, *Hmm, that's strange,* as she rushed out the door.

But then a second drop fell and a third, each one growing bigger until she couldn't call them drops anymore. The cramping became worse than any she'd ever experienced. Still she reasoned it all away. *It's just stress. My body must be going through a change.*

Maybe she even spiritualized her symptoms, deciding that God had a purpose in it all. After all, the gospel account makes it clear that she was a woman of faith. Maybe she told herself, *trials always come before God does something big. Yes, God must be about to do something big in my life. Praise his name! I wonder what he's up to.*

The irony is that God did do something big. This woman's story is still told these two thousand years later. Only the Lord knows how many souls have been awakened to the love of Jesus in its reading and telling. He alone knows how many millions of people have turned their eyes toward heaven because of her. So, yes, praise God for what he did through this woman's life. Let's all stand up and shout it together. Praise God for what he did—*twelve years later.* They were twelve years during which all she knew was that she bled.

I can't begin to imagine what something like that would do to a woman's heart. She was bleeding from her womb. Especially in a first-century woman's mind-set, such bleeding would strike at the core of what makes her a woman. One could almost say it was her very womanhood that spilled from her.

As if that weren't pain enough, in the tradition of her Jewish religion, any woman who was bleeding from her womb was labeled "unclean." No one was allowed to touch a woman who was unclean. Can you even begin to imagine—no one will touch you? The people point their fingers and whisper to each other, "It's that woman there. She's unclean."

I often think of her husband, assuming she had a husband and assuming he didn't leave her as the years multiplied. For her sake, I hope he was more sensitive to her needs than devoted to the Law. I hope she never heard him say, "No, honey. You're not clean." I hope he didn't take his bedding and sleep in the other room. I hope she never felt the dagger a woman must feel when the man she loves pushes her away.

She would have no children during those twelve years. She would have only pain. She would only struggle with the daily mess, the fear of not knowing when it might happen, and the embarrassment of having to rush from the room when it did happen.

So many times she'd scrape hope from the floor and try with everything in her to believe that tomorrow would be a better day. With every new doctor and each new treatment, her heart would soar in expectation—and then crumble to the ground in disappointment when the blood just continued to flow.

She would cry tears with her friends in the day and tears all alone in the night. She would cry out to God and wonder why he was so silent. For twelve long years she would wonder why he was silent.

Be merciful to me, O LORD, for I am in distress;
my eyes grow weak with sorrow,
my soul and my body with grief.
—*Psalm 31:9*

There was a time, of course, before the bleeding, when this precious woman's heart was filled only with dreams and excitement about her future. I picture her in youth, lying awake in the middle of the night, planning her family and debating her children's names. I imagine there was a day when she realized her attractiveness and noticed the smile of boys and wondered which one she would fall in love with and marry. She was so ready to skip into adulthood, believing with all her heart that it was going to be entirely marvelous and thrilling.

But as she sits in the dust of that Galilean street waiting for Jesus to walk by, the wonder that once inspired the bounce in her step now lies crushed by life's hardness. As she desperately plans, *I need only touch the hem of his garment,* all of her youthful plans lie forgotten. Yes, twelve years of bleeding and all that's flowed from it has taken a terrible toll. Hope has turned into desperation. The promise of a future has turned into grabbing for today. Falling to sleep every night with a giggle and a prayer has turned into waking every morning to a tear-stained pillow.

And more than anything, there's the shame. In the wake of each rejection, dirtiness, and pain there has come so very much shame. Oh for a woman's dignity. Oh the nights upon nights that she's cried out to God, "Please, Father, end my shame!"

Do not let the floodwaters engulf me
or the depths swallow me up
or the pit close its mouth over me.
Answer me, O LORD, out of the goodness of your love;
In your great mercy turn to me.
—Psalm 69:15–16

If I may flash-forward to the twenty-first century that you and I live in, we can only thank God that a woman never has to face (at least in the Western world) what this precious woman did. Praise to God for medical advances that make her condition a horror of times past. No, women today don't bleed from their wombs for twelve years, but if you'll allow me to suggest—and I step very lightly—many women do bleed from their hearts.

There are so many things that can cut a woman's heart. There is so much bleeding that goes on in so many ways. There is the blade of love turned sour and the blade of love rejected. Not being a woman, I can't know for sure, but I have a feeling that when a woman offers her heart to a man, it is no small occasion. She puts her life in a man's hands. She takes her most precious and fragile self and says to him, "I trust you with me. I trust you will never break me."

Then comes that day when trust is broken in one way or the other, and a woman's heart is broken along with it. The bleeding begins, and in spite of every effort to pick up the pieces and get on with life, the bleeding continues. In spite of other suitors and everyone's advice and claiming, "All things work together for good," the bleeding doesn't stop. It just goes on. Sometimes for years.

There are other blades as well—some more horrific than others. I know a woman who was violated as a young girl by her father. She was seven when it started and seventeen when she was able to escape. There was more than one pregnancy, and with each one there was an abortion. Her young heart bled all through her young years, just as her woman's heart continues to bleed today.

I once received a letter from a woman whose husband was a pastor. One day he turned his back on her and their three children and walked out the door. He left them all for another man. Yes, I said *man*. And so her heart bleeds.

Then there's the woman who's just been told by the doctor that she can't have children, and the woman who had a mastectomy. As strong and brave as they both are, and as well as everyone thinks they're handling it, deep inside their hearts they bleed.

There's the single mom who struggles to make things work

and the woman who always feels like she doesn't measure up. There's the widow who wakes up alone after thirty years of marriage and the wife who sleeps with a husband who doesn't love her anymore. There's the one who gave the best years of her life to care for her aging parents. Now they're gone, and she's alone—and bleeding.

Yes, we live in an age where women don't bleed from their wombs for twelve terrible years anymore, but so very many quietly bleed from their hearts. Oh Father, have mercy . . . JESUS.

She came up behind him and touched the edge of his cloak and immediately her bleeding stopped.
—*Luke 8:44*

Jesus turned and saw her. "Take heart, daughter," he said, "your faith has healed you." And the woman was healed from that moment.
—*Matthew 9:22*

One touch from Jesus—or should I say one "touching of" Jesus—and those twelve years were no more. Was it faith that moved Jesus that day? There is obviously something to be said for the sureness with which this woman pressed through the crowd toward him. At the same time I tend to think that Jesus was moved even more . . . well . . . simply by her.

He'd created her inmost being. He'd knit her together in her mother's womb. She was his "baby." If I may, she was his little girl. So, all faith aside, I have a feeling that what moved Jesus most was just her.

And I can only guess that it was quite the moment when the two of them stood in the midst of that crushing throng, looking into each other's eyes as if they stood alone. I can only imagine that her mind raced in awe: *He's standing next to a synagogue ruler, and everyone in the crowd wants his attention. But his eyes are only for me. This man is my God—and his eyes are for me.*

I imagine that Jesus, without saying a word, responded through the genuineness in his countenance and the breadth of his kingdom smile: *Yes, most precious woman. Dare to believe it. It's not that I love them any less. It's that I love you. I* AM *who created you—and what matters to me is you.*

Is Jesus moved by your faith today? Do you work hard to keep free from doubt? Do you speak those positive scriptures and struggle to live in the promises of his Word no matter what presses in about you?

Does all that move Jesus? Probably. But there are other guys who can answer that better than me. I just tend to think he's more moved by you. You're his baby, his little girl—and what moves the heart of Jesus is *you*.

And so he whispers into the quiet of your soul . . .

I created you, my precious one. I saw your unformed body long before you came to be, just as I see you now. And all your days were written in my book a long, long time ago.

I love you, precious woman—just the way you are. Oh that you would truly believe that it truly is that simple. Even with all those feelings you feel bad about and the times you think you let me down. Even with all those things you think make you lesser (but really don't). Even with that "you know what" no one else knows about—I love you, my child. You've captured my heart. I've never for one moment felt any other way.

And you must never again think you are an accident. You must never again think no one cares. I planned you. I desired and willed you. I held you in my heart long ago, just as I hold you so closely today.

I have known your suffering, precious daughter. Not one of your cries went unheard. Every moment of bleeding took the wind from me, and every heartache broke my heart as well.

I was not the author of those terrible things that happened. They were not my perfect desire. But I AM the one who redeems them all. Look closely, and you will see that promise alive and living in my eyes.

May I have the honor of wiping away your every tear?

Let me reach deep into your heart—yes, that's right—and wipe them all away.

There you go, my child. Let yesterday be no more. Release it from your grasp, and together let us live today unto tomorrow. Unto forever I AM yours today, and I AM yours tomorrow.

I love you, my precious one. I love you, I love you.
JESUS.

The LORD appeared to us in the past, saying:
"I have loved you with an everlasting love;
I have drawn you with loving-kindness."
—Jeremiah 31:3

"I know the plans I have for you," declares the LORD,
"plans to prosper you and not to harm you, plans to give
you hope and a future."
—Jeremiah 29:11

As the Father has loved me, so I have loved you.
Now remain in my love.
—John 15:9

I love you.
JESUS.

On a Sabbath Jesus was teaching in one of the synagogues, and a woman was there who had been crippled by a spirit for eighteen years. She was bent over and could not straighten up at all. When Jesus saw her, he called her forward and said to her, "Woman, you are set free from your infirmity." Then he put his hands on her, and immediately she straightened up and praised God.

—Luke 13:10–13

"Come to Me"

*I*f I may, I'd like to begin the telling of this woman's story by painting a specific picture of Jesus' compassion and passion of heart. Journey with me to the day when he stood before a Galilean multitude and cried, no doubt, from the bottom of his heart . . .

> *Come to me, all you who are weary and burdened,*
> *and I will give you rest.*
> *Take my yoke upon you and learn from me,*
> *for I am gentle and humble in heart,*
> *and you will find rest for your souls.*
> *—Matthew 11:28–29*

JESUS.

Those words are some of Jesus' most widely known and beloved words—and for very good reasons. First, they are so tender, gracious, and genuine. They reach toward us with care and deep understanding of our most basic human need. They are filled with such promise that we find ourselves drawn to them "as the deer pants for streams of water" (Psalm 42:1).

There's a second reason why I believe those words resonate so strongly in our hearts. I may be wrong, but I have a feeling that they affirm the kind of man that we know—deep down inside—Jesus truly is.

There's so much conflicting teaching about Jesus. One teaching emphasizes his mercy and grace. Another paints him as consumed with righteous indignation. Still another speaks of him only in his majesty and power. We can easily become confused.

And think of the film portrayals of Jesus. In one film, Jesus is perpetually walking through meadows and playing with children. In another he's an angry young man belting out condemnation. In yet another we see him aloof and detached, pious and ethereal. This is how a lot of sculpture and art also portrays him.

Then there are those lines in our Bibles that tend to shake us up a bit. "You snakes!" (Matthew 23:33). "Are you still so dull?" (Matthew 15:16). "It is not right to take the children's bread and toss it to their dogs" (Mark 7:27). *Taken out of context,* those scriptures can make Jesus appear to be hard, unfeeling, and maybe even downright mean.

So when Jesus looks into our hearts through the pages of the gospel and whispers, "I am gentle and humble in heart," our souls shout, "Yes!" We are not denying his majesty and power or discounting his righteousness. Our excitement doesn't suggest that

Jesus isn't God before whom we bow our faces in worship and honor.

It simply means that Jesus is good and that I can trust my life to his care. It means he's safe and won't harm me. It means he's . . . well . . . Jesus, and deep inside ourselves—through the sovereign work of the Holy Spirit and in a way that transcends mere intellectual comprehension—we just *know* what that name means.

JESUS.

There's a third reason we're so drawn to those words that is quite possibly the biggest reason of all. I believe they reach into the core of one of our deepest human longings. They whisper, "This is what you're *really* looking for." When all the satisfactions we seek are boiled down to their bared essence, this is what we find: I'm speaking of rest. *Rest for the soul.*

So few of us ever experience true rest in our souls. We hunt for it in many places—achievement, relationships, entertainment, and comforts. We dance around it by keeping our lives filled with activity, rushing from email to cell phone to lunch with Patty and coffee with Cheryl. Even in church circles, we scurry from conference to Bible study to choir practice. Don't get me wrong—these are all fulfilling and fruitful activities. They just don't bring rest to the soul.

And so often they are all just busyness for the sake of busyness, pursued in the hope of silencing the longing for rest. Deep inside, a person wrestles, *Whatever you do, don't let yourself be still.*

Quiet becomes the enemy, because it is in the quiet that the longing overwhelms. "Oh Father in heaven, to have rest in my soul."

It must have been quite a day two thousand years ago when Jesus uttered that tender invitation, "Come to me." By way of background, he'd been pressing from one Galilean village to another. He knew that time was limited as each passing day carried him closer to the cross. He knew that every sunset meant that the opportunity to reach his precious children was slipping away.

This was Jesus' desperation, if you will. This was his life's passion as a man. Singularly he lived to please his Father, and intricately intertwined within that dedication, he lived to save his children—you and me.

This was Jesus' excitement. This was what made his heart skip a beat and filled his dreams at night. This was what got him on his feet every morning to get out there no matter what opposition he faced. He was a man in passionate pursuit of those precious people two thousand years ago, and of you and me today.

Do you not say, "Four months more and then the harvest"? I tell you, open your eyes and look at the fields! They are ripe for harvest.
—John 4:35

Jesus said to them, "My Father is always at his work to this very day, and I, too, am working."
—John 5:17

JESUS.

To understand Jesus' passion a little more, consider your own heart for your own little one. Think about every hope and desire you ever had for him or her. Think about how far you'd go for your children to realize their very best in life. Take your sacrifice and your instinct to shield them from pain. Multiply it all a billion, trillion times, and you've got Jesus.

You've got Jesus teaching in the marketplaces and synagogues. You've got Jesus on his knees in the dirt with the lepers and cripples. You've got him with his arms wrapped around the shoulders of the brokenhearted, crying heavenly tears for every brokenness he sees. In his divine understanding, he knows each and every one of them by name. Parental passion is a literal bonfire ablaze in his heart.

When he saw the crowds, he had compassion on them, because they were harassed and helpless, like sheep without a shepherd.
—Matthew 9:36

I have engraved you on the palms of my hands.
—Isaiah 49:16

So he rolls up his sleeves and "hits the pavement." He shrugs free of every thought toward self and pours the entirety of his mind, body, heart, and soul into each precious child. Day after day, village after village, with urgency and zeal he reaches toward them. His fervent desire is to lift their burdens. His impassioned purpose is to give them rest for their souls. His every teaching, miracle, and drop of sweat is a display of love such as none of them have ever imagined—*and still they turn and walk away.*

Oh how that must have pained his heart. He alone knows the hope and future that could be theirs. He alone knows the fullness of rest that lies before them, free for the taking. And he alone knows the weight of sin and guilt that buries their souls and crushes their hearts. If they would only come, he would sweep it all away.

I picture Jesus that "come to me" day with his heart just shattered by it all. I imagine tears flooding the wells of his eyes and dripping into the sand about his feet. He extends his arms. "I'm gentle and humble in heart." He drops to his knees. "I'll give you rest for your souls." He breaks before the people in open heartache and a depth of compassion that is so beyond that of mere men, a compassion that could only come from the heart of God himself. It's as if he pleads with all of his being . . .

Oh my precious ones, come to me. Come live in my embrace where there is only goodness and salvation, where there is only warmth in righteousness and pureness of peace. Oh how I long that you would come and live in me, high and lifted

*up above the weight of this broken world and all the broken
things that bear down on you.*

*Are you weary? Come! Are you burdened? Come! Taste of
my gentleness. My heart lies humble before you. I offer you
me—and you'll find rest in your soul—that wondrous prize
you long for. As you come and fill your heart with me, just
as my heart is filled with you, I promise you will find rest for
your soul.*

JESUS.

Thus was the heart of Jesus. Thus was the man who was teaching in the synagogue that day while a woman "who had been crippled by a spirit for eighteen years" looked on. As Luke records, "She was bent over and could not straighten up at all." Still she watched, and she listened—to Jesus.

I think most of us have a specific picture of this woman in our imaginations, as we've all seen an elderly person with advanced osteoporosis pass us on the street or in the grocery store aisle. Personally I have a very tender heart for elderly people, so to see someone stooped and struggling always hurts. Most especially if that someone's a woman. Even more if she's a woman alone.

We don't know for sure that this Galilean woman's "infirmity," as Jesus called it, was osteoporosis. We don't even know how old, or maybe even young, she was. The gospel account doesn't share those details, and it's always a mistake to presume.

What we do know is that she was crippled "by a spirit." Maybe it's just my ever-practical perspective, but I don't necessarily think that means something mystical occurred. I don't see it as some black figure swooping down one day and zapping her in the spine. Those filthy oppressors tend to operate in a much more subtle fashion.

I could be wrong, but I'd like to suggest that this precious woman's infirmity developed little by little, one inch at a time, going almost unnoticed by everyone around her. I'd like to suggest that the crippling overtook her in tiny increments. As if pebbles were piled on her back one at a time, there came a burden here and a burden there over so many years of burdened living that one day she was "bent over" with the weight of them all.

You know that cliché "You look like you have the weight of the world on your shoulders"? Have you ever seen anyone like that? Have you ever seen what the weight of life and the weariness of repeated hurt and struggle—even aloneness—can do to a person's physicality over time?

I know a woman in her early forties whose shoulders are hunched and whose back is bowed. The diagnosis? Years of depression.

I once lived next door to an older man whose wife criticized and belittled him continually. Everything was his fault, and every move he made was wrong. I would often see him working in his garden, and then I would see his wife banging on the window, pointing at weeds he'd missed or a bush that wasn't trimmed the way she wanted. I often heard her yelling though the walls, cursing at him and saying terrible things. Sometimes he would come over to my house to get away from it all. Sometimes he would pour his heart out and just cry. But then he'd have to go back home—and the badgering would continue.

Over the years of being neighbors, I saw him change. He got slower and slower, and more and more quiet. His shoulders slumped, and his head hung low. He would lean on whatever was near, as if he would fall if he didn't. Sometimes it seemed that he could hardly breathe. There wasn't anything wrong with him physically. *It was the constant beating he took in his heart.*

That's the way I tend to see this woman who'd been crippled by a spirit. The crush of a lot of who-knows-what—doubt, fear, abuse, hopelessness—taking its terrible toll on her body. Maybe like my neighbor, she was married to an "enemy." Over the decades of their marriage, perhaps he made her feel she could never do anything right. Maybe everything was always her fault and she could never measure up. Perhaps he picked her apart and nailed her every wrong and had her convinced she was worthless. Maybe there were even worse abuses. After all, who really knows what goes on behind closed doors?

I knew a young woman whose husband cheated on her openly. Worse yet, he told her that her inadequacy was to blame. He had her so bewitched, and being a man who sat in church every Sunday with a Bible under his arm, he continually threatened her with scriptures such as "God hates divorce." So she stuck it out, certain that as she prayed, he would turn around. It went on for years—years during which she became more and more crippled. He never did turn around. Oh Father, have mercy.

Who knows what this Galilean woman's life had been like and why she would be crippled for so many years? Who knows what her daddy did or didn't do, instead of being a real father? Who knows how many disappointments and hardships and failures beat her down?

Or maybe she was just plain "life weary." Life can be hard, and many of us seem to get more than our fair share of hardships. Others of us are just more fragile.

You love; they die. You give your life to them; they go away. You get excited about this and you try that, but nothing ever seems to turn out right. You stick your neck out only to get hurt over and again. A bad decision leads to more bad decisions. A day of aloneness turns into years of being alone—a day somehow turns into a lifetime.

Big and small, the cruelties of life come, and the enemy "spirit" misses no opportunity to wrench every one of them deep into our souls. He jams them into our hearts like a million tiny needles and hangs them before our minds' eyes. One by one, he heaps them on our backs like boulders. He hooks them into our understanding and ties them around our necks. He stacks them—one failure at a time, one loss at a time, one disappointment and abuse at a time—until a woman's face is bent to the floor.

When Jesus saw her, he called her forward." He must have spotted her through the lattice barrier that customarily separated the women from the men in the synagogues. It was a barrier that kept the women "in the back." It kept them in the shadows. It kept them in the place of "lesser."

I wonder what the moment was like. I wonder if Jesus was passionately teaching, then looked up and just suddenly stopped. I wonder if their eyes met, and I wonder what he saw in hers that made him stop. Yes, perhaps it wasn't so much that her back was bent. Maybe it was more the yearning he saw in her eyes.

She was his precious child. He "knew" her by name. Indeed, he was the God who'd named her. So as he looks up and sees what the weight of life lived in a broken world had done to her, I imagine he felt like a knife was piercing his heart. I can see tears filling the wells of his eyes, draining down his cheeks into the web of his beard. I imagine the whole room looking about, wondering why Jesus had stopped. But he pays them no mind. In that moment she fills the fullness of his heart.

In all their distress he too was distressed,
and the angel of his presence saved them.
In his love and mercy he redeemed them;
he lifted them up and carried them all the days of old.
—Isaiah 63:9

I imagine Jesus stepping out from behind the Torah scroll. He stops being a teacher and becomes a man—a man who is God who is her every hope. He reaches his hand to her in a gesture that whispers, *Come to me.* He calls her forward. *You who are weary and burdened.* He invites her to his side. *You'll find rest for your soul.*

Come out from behind the lattice, precious one. You're not lesser to me. Come to the front—to where I AM. Don't be afraid. Don't worry about what others will think. Just come, my child. Come to me.

JESUS.

I can guess she didn't respond right away. I can guess she stood frozen for a time. After all, Jesus was asking her to go where no woman of that day was ever supposed to go—especially a woman like her, bent and crippled and probably not feeling like the most worthy person in town.

Yet she is the one his eyes are calling. His eyes make her feel as if she's the only one in the room. And there's so much hope in them. There's so much expectation and promise. There's a warmth in their gaze that says *I love you, dear woman; I love you.*

And so she musters every tattered shred of confidence she can and takes a step. It's hard for her to move her legs, and every effort sends shocks of pain, but for the first time in so long there's excitement in her heart. She takes another step and another, coming and coming to Jesus.

She strains to lift her head to see how much farther she has to go. She shuffles past this one and says "Excuse me" to that one. She stops to catch her breath. She forces another step and then another . . . *I've just got to get to Jesus!*

I imagine Jesus moving toward her as well, his hand extended in gentlemanly care. *Come,* his eyes continue to whisper, beckoning her nearer and nearer. Exhausted, she finally reaches him and falls into his embrace, just as he slides his strong arm beneath the weight of her shoulders. She begins to cry, feeling exposed and vulnerable. Jesus is crying too. She can feel his tears dripping onto the bow of her back.

He wants to look into her eyes, and so he goes to his knees. He takes her hands and squeezes them in gentle assurance. He lifts her chin. He brushes back the hair that has hung over her countenance like a shroud and concealed her loveliness for too many years.

She looks into the fullness of his face. He smiles just as tears, now of joy, flood his eyes even more. He reaches his hand over her most crippled place. His hand is so calm and sure. He lays it on the center of her back, and its very warmth makes her knees feel like water. Gently he presses. It's as if he presses past all the crippledness—*and touches her heart.*

"Woman, you are set free," his lips whisper, and her every burden is melted away. With one stroke, he erases it *all.*

Suddenly she can breathe again! She hasn't been able to fully breathe for so long. She lifts her head—the pain is gone. It's been eighteen years, and now the pain is gone! She raises her eyes and lifts her face. She stretches her arms toward the ceiling in praise. She looks to Jesus as fresh tears explode, and he just smiles and smiles as she rises straighter and straighter, free of the weight, free of the weariness—free to live in rest, in him.

JESUS.

These two thousand years later, Jesus turns that same smile toward you and me. He whispers through the tunnel of time, reaching his hand toward your heart just as he reached his hand so deeply into that precious woman's heart and life that day . . .

I love you, my child, and I say, "Come to me." I AM he who gives you rest. I AM your place of rest. Oh you who fill my heart to overflowing, I AM living rest, and my rest is for you.

Be wearied no more—just come. Lay your every burden down. Let the days of struggling to breathe come to an end. Let the days of striving be no more.

I know that life has been hard and that it so often seemed to be so much harder for you than for others. I know those times when you wondered if I cared—you wondered what benefit there was in praying. I know those times when you stood tall in church and raised your hands in worship just like everyone else, but deep inside you felt bent to the floor. Inside you were crying and crumbling under so many burdens that you didn't understand. I know how alone and abandoned you've felt.

Oh precious one, I know, and what I say to you is, "Come." Come into the embrace of my every grace, and enter the rest I desire for your soul. Place every burden here at my feet. Come, lay your weariness down. I'm gentle, my child. I'm humble in my heart. And my promise to you is rest for your soul. I love you, my precious one. I love you.
JESUS.

He brought me out into a spacious place. He rescued me because he delighted in me.
—Psalm 18:19

I love you.
JESUS.

57

At dawn [Jesus] appeared again in the temple courts,

where all the people gathered around him,

and he sat down to teach them.

The teachers of the law and the Pharisees

brought in a woman caught in adultery.

They made her stand before the group and said to Jesus,

"Teacher, this woman was caught in the act of adultery.

In the Law Moses commanded us to stone such women.

Now what do you say?"

—John 8:2–5

"Neither Do I Condemn You"

*I*t is no great revelation to say that sleeping with a man to whom you weren't married wasn't exactly the safest thing a woman could do within the religious culture of first-century Israel. At the very least, it meant scorn and humiliation. At the very worst, it meant execution by stoning.

So the question begs to be asked, "Why would she do it?" With her entire future at stake and so much to lose—even her very life—what prize lay within that man's arms that would compel her to take such risk? What treasure did she think she would find in his kiss? What would drive any woman to place herself in such danger?

The human heart is so complex and bottomless in its passions and needs that I can guess there are many answers to those questions. At the same time, I don't think I'd be too out of bounds to boil them all down to one word, one reality, one all-encompassing longing that just might be the most consuming human longing of all: *love*.

To love and be loved. To find and give love. To rest and live in a love that inspires, protects, and fulfills. Truly nothing of human desire can be more overpowering than the yearning for love.

It can cause the strongest among us to crumble in need. It can derail the most driven and focused and compel the most sensible and grounded person to act like a fool. It can impel the most God-seeking believer to do what he knows he ought not to do. And it can drive a woman—this precious, first-century woman—to risk her very life.

Knowing the intensity of the power of love, a king named Solomon sat down a thousand years before this woman made that dangerous decision, and he wrote these Spirit-inspired words:

Daughters of Jerusalem, I charge you
by the gazelles and by the does of the field:
Do not arouse or awaken love until the time is right.
—*Song of Songs 2:7 NIV & NLT*

Solomon's words are sage counsel to be sure. In God's perfect timing, the right time for love will be revealed. In God's perfect plan, his spouse of choice will be known. In a perfect world full of perfect people, a man and a woman wait patiently for his timing and plan to come together. They wait for God to show them whom to marry, and they wait for God to show them when. Then together they grasp hands, skip into the sunset, and live the rest of their lives happily ever after.

That's a wonderful scenario, and I've actually met a few couples who have successfully walked it. I've heard guys say, "My wife is the only woman I've ever kissed." I've had women tell me, "My husband is the only man I ever dated."

I praise God for such stories. I praise God that there are actually people out there who have been able to live that ideal. But in a world that is far from perfect and filled with imperfect people (kind of like me), we all have to acknowledge that those couples are extremely rare.

I recently had lunch with a friend whom I hadn't seen in several years. She had married just six months before, and I wanted to hear how she was doing. Before the waiter could even bring our coffee, she was awash in sobs. "I've made a terrible mistake," she said through her tears. "I don't know what I'm going to do." She'd married a man in haste, as her midthirties bore down upon her. Oh the mistakes that have been made under the pressure to act "before it's too late."

We've all known both men and women, young and old, who simply cannot be alone. They always seem to have a new boyfriend or girlfriend on their arms. They're continually "falling in love" with someone new.

I will never forget a fifty-something widow who once cried in my arms. After the death of her husband, she got involved with a man who abused her in ways she didn't verbalize, but she couldn't bring herself to turn him out. His abuse was better, it seemed, than being alone. Oh the heartaches that have flowed from not wanting to be alone.

Then there is the heartache that comes from just plain loneliness. There's a loneliness that can come when a person is literally alone, and there's a loneliness that can come even in the middle of a relationship. I can't imagine the pain of being married and "alone," as so many are—alone in your thoughts, alone in your heart, alone in hopes and dreams—feeling like a stranger to the person who sleeps next to you.

The yearning for love hooks into that wife's loneliness, just as the desire to be desired scratches at its door. Together they turn a coworker's smile into something much more. His casual greeting seems filled with innuendo. A quick stop to say hello turns into coffee, which turns into lunch, which turns into a whole lot more . . . and love is aroused when it should have been run from. Maybe it's aroused again and again.

Yes, the hunger for human love may very easily be the most penetrating power in human experience. It is the proverbial tiger by the tail. In its bittersweet grip, countless hearts have awakened love when it wasn't love's time. Many others have awakened what wasn't truly love but felt enough like love—and in the end, it only stole one's love away.

Halle Berry, who is one of the world's most successful and celebrated beauties, once said in an interview, "I know what it's like to hunger so much for a human touch that you throw your dignity away." Sometimes, for whatever reason, the heart feels so empty and wants for so much that love "in its time" is traded for love anytime, at any cost, and in any way.

JESUS.

And so two thousand years ago, a woman whose name we don't know lies in the quiet of night beside a man to whom she's not married. The gospel story calls her "a woman caught in adultery." Of course I have no way of knowing her mind or heart, but I prefer to call her a woman in want of love.

Who was this precious woman, and what led her to this "caught in adultery" day? Perhaps she was one among the much too lonely. Perhaps she had fought against it for years, doing everything she could to busy herself and be strong. But a man can sense loneliness in a woman's demeanor, and the wrong kind of man can be so very dangerous, opting to prey instead of protect.

Maybe her man was that wrong kind of man. Maybe he saw the weakness and chose his time, flattering her here, and "caring" just enough there. Maybe his attention felt so good that she ignored the warning signs and dropped her guard—and one day woke up where she'd always promised she would never, ever be.

On the other hand, maybe he was the "right" man. Perhaps

he valued her and treated her with gentleness and care—the way her husband had vowed to treat her. Indeed, he was the kind of man she thought her husband was on that wondrous day when the two of them stood together beneath their wedding canopy. They smashed the goblet and laughed and kissed, and she believed with all her heart that their every tomorrow would be lived in this same, wondrous way.

I've known many women who woke up one day and thought, *Where did my husband go? This man I live with is not the man I married. How could I not have seen these things beforehand? I was praying and seeking, so why didn't God show me?*

Truly, I've heard that story so many times that it almost rings in my ear as epidemic. There's a friend from San Antonio who's now alone with a baby. There's the friend from Oregon who thanks God they never had a baby. There's the friend from just up the street whose walls have so many fist holes in them it's only a matter of time before she's next.

Not a one of them saw it coming. Oh there were odd things that happened here and there, but they were easily explained away. "He's under a lot of stress." "He's having trouble at work." "Everyone is entitled to his moods."

Who knows if this woman caught in adultery couldn't tell a similar story? Who knows what fear in marriage or what emotional neglect may have driven such a stake in her heart that she fell into the warmth of more gracious arms? Yes, maybe he was a good man, this man with whom she lay so peacefully. Maybe he was the man she should have met and would have married if only she'd known. Maybe he was a man who *really* loved her. Maybe he was a man who truly cared.

Then again, perhaps this woman was, well . . . I think of what Halle Berry said. Perhaps, for whatever reason, her "hunger for a human touch" was just too much. Perhaps she tried to overcome it with everything in her, and perhaps she even succeeded many times. But no matter how much she prayed, the need never waned. Instead it was her strength that waned with each thought of its fulfillment.

It's easy to stand at a self-righteous distance and wonder how anyone could do such a thing. It's even easy to look at oneself in the mirror and ask, *How could I have done that?* But you know, in the complex and powerful web of human emotion and desire, it isn't always that simple.

So there comes the day when this precious woman sheds her robe. One can only imagine the mixture of excitement and fear and the knowing deep in her heart that "as right as this feels, this doesn't feel right at all." She folds her robe carefully. She drapes it over a chair. She turns toward the man, and though she's counted the cost in her mind over and over, though she's held out and held on and tried so hard to do what she knows God wants her to do . . . she gives herself over to his arms.

Oh most costly moment. The next day's rising sun gives rise to so much conflict and confusion within her. Even as she lay in the quiet of his embrace, she beats herself up and promises never again. Later that day she'll have to face all the faces in her life as if nothing at all has changed.

But something has changed, and as a result, some things can never be the same—ever again. No matter how much she prays for forgiveness and no matter how much she knows she's forgiven, "the moment" is still there. No matter how determined she is that it will never happen again, and no matter how much he agrees, and "oh well, life goes on," it's still there.

What's worse—and what is a total surprise to her—is that her desire only grows. She'd intended that her sampling of desire's pleasures would make it go away, but instead it became a monster. She finds herself unable to stop thinking about him. She finds herself reasoning, *Maybe just once more*. She begs God for forgiveness and for strength anew. She commits and recommits. She busies herself and avoids him as much as she can.

But that feeling that stirs up so much feeling inside her just won't go away. The memories, the intimacy, the acceptance, and the love—they all cry to be revisited. The aloneness she'd suffered under—except for that one moment with him—now overwhelms her even more. Only in his arms did she feel valued and complete, and so, in spite of all determination to do things God's way, she turns to him again. "Just one more time" turns into many more times. It turns into a lifestyle. Perhaps it turns into years.

There's yet another possibility: maybe this precious woman was simply "on the run." Perhaps her running into men's arms had little to do with looking for love or feeling alone or neglected. Maybe it was because she had been so terribly hurt by something so deeply injurious that she was frantically running toward anything that would medicate her pain.

I know a woman whose fiancé was killed at war. They'd met in Bible college and had shared a dream of working together in the mission field, serving God and reaching out in his name. They did everything God's way, never crossing physical lines, while most other students did. They were so very much in love and excited about the work they "just knew" was God's purpose and plan for their lives.

With that surety deep in their hearts, they had little fear when he took up arms and went away. He would do his duty in commitment to his country, while she researched and planned for their missionary future. The letters went back and forth, and both were counting the days until he would come home and they could carry on as they had been. Together.

Then one day when she was visiting his family, a military vehicle pulled up to the curb. There were men in it, and they had a letter with them. It was an official letter, written to his father and mother. It was the letter no father or mother ever wants to receive and that no fiancée wants to see them receive. Just like that, the dream, the promise, and the future of a young college couple who wanted only to serve God with both of their lives was no more.

My friend went into a tailspin. She tossed out God and all of his disciplines that had been her greatest pleasure to enjoy. She ran from bottle to drug to man to men. She ran to many men. She ran for a long time. She was just so terribly hurt. Oh so understandably, she was deeply broken and angry.

So who really knows what was going on inside this precious woman's life and heart two thousand years ago? It's so easy to turn up our noses at her—and women like her—in churchy arrogance. It's so easy to write them off as weak. How quickly we grab God's grace for our own lives but think condescendingly toward others. And in doing so, we unwittingly become exactly like those Pharisees who treated "the woman caught in adultery" as something less than the sinners they themselves were.

> *As it is written: "There is no one righteous,*
> *not even one. . . ." For* all *have sinned and*
> *fall short of the glory of God.*
> —*Romans 3:10, 23*

Oh Father, forgive us.
JESUS.

They made her stand before the group and said to Jesus,
"Teacher, this woman was caught in the act of adultery.
In the Law Moses commanded us to stone such women.
Now what do you say?"
—*John 8:3–5*

Other than Jesus' trial and crucifixion, I don't think there's a more vivid account of godless cruelty in all the gospels. It is truly mind-bending that grown, educated, civilized men—not to mention that they were praying men, devoted to God—can treat a woman the way they treated this precious woman.

It is a screaming testimony to the horror of pride and arrogance and determination to be right. It literally shouts that the sin of all sins is religious self-righteousness. Truly, it is the most dangerous and godless sin there is.

One can only imagine the thoughts that must have raced through Jesus' mind and the feelings that must have flooded his heart when he saw his precious "girl" so appallingly manhandled and terrorized. This may be my own imagination, but I would like to suggest what some might think is sacrilege. I would like to suggest that in Jesus' human nature and manly instinct to protect and defend—especially a *woman*—his first impulse that day was to roll up his sleeves and teach those guys a lesson.

After all, as a man, Jesus is the perfection of masculine integrity, righteousness, justice, and compassion, and no true man could stand and do nothing in the face of such atrocity. Jesus stands as the living personification of salvation, refuge, "strong tower," and "deliverer." Indeed his very name means "God Saves," and if anyone needed to be saved in this ugliest of human moments, it was this precious woman who was so unable to save herself.

> *I call to the LORD, who is worthy of praise,*
> *and I am saved from my enemies.*
> *—2 Samuel 22:4*

> *You are a shield around me, O LORD;*
> *you bestow glory on me and lift up my head. . . .*
> *Arise, O LORD!*
> *Deliver me, O my God!*
> *Strike all my enemies on the jaw;*
> *break the teeth of the wicked.*
> *—Psalm 3:3, 7*

JESUS!

Surely what met Jesus' eyes that day was an affront to everything he was and everything he stood for. I can guess there are few things that rile his holy wrath like violence toward women, so surely it gave rise to his every manly instinct. Surely his first impulse was to cut loose in righteous and justified indignation.

But the mercy of Jesus is so remarkably inclusive. It is a mystery that surpasses human comprehension: he actually feels the same love for these remarkably ghastly men that he feels for her. It bends the mind, but his hope for those men is just as high as it is for the woman they threw at his feet.

There is more:

> *The fruit of the Spirit is love, joy, peace,*
> *patience, kindness, goodness, faithfulness,*
> *gentleness and* self-control.
> *Against such things there is no law.*
> —*Galatians 5:22–23*

These qualities are the end result of the Holy Spirit alive and living in a person's life—and there was no life in all of history that was filled with God's Spirit more than Jesus'. So in fullness of godly *self-control*, he restrains his first impulse. He relaxes the fist that he's so entitled to let fly, and he saves her, instead, in his Father's way. He saves her in the way that tries to save them too:

> *"If anyone of you is without sin, let him be the first to*
> *throw a stone at her." . . . At this, those who heard began to*
> *go away one at a time, the older ones first, until only Jesus*
> *was left, with the woman still standing there.*
> —*John 8:7, 9*

Can you imagine the silence that must have blanketed the courtyard when it was just the two of them? I picture her trying to gain control of her emotions, trying to restrain her sobs. She would have been so afraid, facing these men with rocks in their fists and hearing their murderous threats. She would have been terrified.

I picture Jesus taking off his cloak and covering her. It was early in the morning, and she would have been so cold. I picture him taking her into his arms and holding her. Those arms were her champion, and now they are her comforter. I picture him holding her and not letting go and then holding her even more.

And in the silence of those moments, I wonder if Jesus didn't think of his own mother. People said she was an adulteress too. I wonder if his thoughts didn't travel back to the times he saw her suffer insults and scorn, and possibly even worse. I wonder if there were times, as a boy or even a young man, when he'd held her in his arms just as he held this precious woman, and she had cried too. Yes, I can't help but think that Jesus had thoughts of his mother—thoughts that made his heart rend for this woman all the more.

JESUS.

Who knows how much time may have passed as they stood together that day. We read these gospel stories, presuming the moments follow quickly one upon another—but who really knows? She had been in fear for her life. They had dragged her through the streets. They wanted to kill her. One word from Jesus, and it would have been so.

Who knows how long it took for her fear to subside or even

before she could stop shaking? Who knows how much time passed before she could even look up or stand on her own?

And so Jesus holds her tightly in his arms as long as she needs him. Then in fullness of sensitivity, in a voice warm as honey, he utters the words at exactly the right time: "Woman, where are they?"

I picture her crumbling with emotion all over again and Jesus holding her even tighter. Maybe he whispers over her shoulder, "Has no one condemned you?"

"No one, sir," as she cries all the more.

"Then neither do I condemn you."

The tears stream down her cheeks as he holds and holds her.

"Go now and leave your life of sin."

JESUS.

The Pharisees had asked Jesus, "Now what do you say?" What do you say, Jesus, to a woman who has done things that make her wish she could have those moments back and live them very differently? What do you say, Jesus, to a woman who has done things that make her feel like she's less than what a woman ought to be?

What do you say, Jesus, to a woman who wonders if she hasn't ruined everything for herself and even for others—if she hasn't thrown away her future and every possibility of tasting blessing at your Father's hand?

What do you say to a woman whose heart carries regret and shame and who can't seem to shake free of the longings that draw her into failure, no matter how hard she tries or how much she prays? What do you say, Jesus? Now what do you say!? . . .

I love you, *is what I say, my child. I love you with all my heart.*

There is nothing that can separate you from that. It is an unchanging, unshakable reality, and there is nothing you've ever done or ever will do that can even lessen that love, let alone cause me to turn away.

I love you, my child, pure and simple. Take that into the deepest place of your heart and hold it closely—even, believe it or not, in your sin. In fact, hold it tighter and closer in your sin than at any other time. Hold it closer to your sin than to anything else. For it is my love for you—expressed in my shed blood—that washes it all away.

Truly, my child, "Neither do I condemn you." You are my child, and it is all *erased away.*

I was there when you did what you wish you hadn't done, and you know what? I loved you. I was there when you promised you'd never do it again, and you know what? I loved you. I have been there for every moment of both victory and failure, and I have only loved you in the middle of it all.

I understand the yearning for love, my child. No one understands it more. I'm the one who gave my life that I might enjoy love's beauty and wonder—with you. I gave my life, precious woman, that I might enjoy you. So yes, I understand the yearning for love. I understand you.

Now go, my child, and sin no more. Be free and know that I love you no matter what. Know that I await you with my arms open wide and with my heart beating in anticipation.

Forgetting the things that are behind, just move forward. You are my beloved. If you could only see my smile, you would really, deeply know that my smile is because of you.

There is now no condemnation
for those who are in Christ Jesus.
—Romans 8:1

I am a rose of Sharon, a lily of the valleys.
—Song of Songs 2:1

Jesus said to her, "Your sins are forgiven."
—Luke 7:48

I love you.
JESUS.

When they came to the home of the synagogue ruler, Jesus saw a commotion, with people crying and wailing loudly. He went in and said to them, "Why all this commotion and wailing? The child is not dead but asleep."

But they laughed at him.

After he put them all out, he took the child's father and mother and the disciples who were with him and went in where the child was. He took her by the hand and said to her, "Talitha, koum!" (which means, "Little girl, I say to you, get up!"). Immediately the girl stood up and walked around (she was twelve years old). At this they were completely astonished.

—Mark 5:38–42

CHAPTER FIVE

"Talitha, Koum!"

She was just a little girl. A girl of twelve. The little girl was dead. *Until she met Jesus.*

Like most of our gospel stories so far, this one, too, is very well known. It begins with a father—a synagogue ruler named Jairus—who has just lost his daughter. He pushes through a Galilean throng and throws himself at Jesus' feet. He pleads with him, "My daughter has just died. But come and put your hand on her, and she will live" (Matthew 9:18).

Jesus follows Jairus to his home, which is now filled with mourners. He turns to them and speaks that infamous line, "The girl is not dead but asleep." They all have a good laugh—*at the Son of the living God*—and the next thing they know, the girl is on her feet. Glory to the name of Jesus!

I'm going to guess that when this story is taught, just as in the story of the woman with the issue of blood, the emphasis is generally on *faith*. In Luke's account, Jesus encourages Jairus, saying,

"Don't be afraid; just *believe*" (8:50). Couple those words with "the girl is not dead but asleep," and you'll find classic lessons in "speaking life" and speaking "in faith." You'll find a living example of Hebrews 11:1, which defines faith as being sure of what we hope for and certain of what we do not see.

Those lessons are wonderful and immeasurably valuable for "without faith it is impossible to please God" (Hebrews 11:6). But what of this precious little girl at the center of those spiritual lessons? What of this girl who lay so tragically still? Who was this child who lived two thousand years ago? What was her little life like—before? And what horrible thing came and stole it away?

Talitha was her name. Well, not really. But it's what Jesus said to her, and besides, it just sounds so little-girl lovely that I'd like to take that liberty . . .

Talitha's daddy loved her so much. It was very evident on that day when she ceased to be. Here he was a synagogue ruler, and he prostrated himself before Jesus in the dirt (see Luke 8:41). He abandoned all pride of position and begged Jesus in front of the entire town. He even begged for something that would have sounded so shocking and utterly foolish to most everyone's ears— he actually asked Jesus to make her alive again.

That's how much Talitha's daddy loved his little girl. He didn't care about his reputation or status or even holding the town's respect. He didn't care that everyone was watching and that those who weren't would know before sunset. He was not concerned that most of his Pharisee friends thought Jesus was a fake and that they would surely hold it against him. On this day that was the most dreaded of daddy days—this day when all of a daddy's love and resources are entirely helpless to save—all he cared about was his precious little girl. All he cared about was Talitha.

I wonder if anyone laughed that day when Talitha's daddy pleaded between his sobs, "Put your hand on her, and she will live" (Matthew 9:18). I wonder if anyone laughed out loud in a burst of astonishment or perhaps turned in disgust and harrumphed away. I wonder if Talitha's father heard them through his sobbing and begging. Or maybe one of his friends took him by the arm and said, "Get up now! You're making a fool of yourself."

We can't know whether those kinds of things happened or not, but to Tailtha's father, they wouldn't have mattered in the least. He loved his little girl, and all he wanted was to have her back. To that end he would do whatever it took, no matter what. He would beg Jesus "till the cows came home," and it didn't matter who saw him or what anyone thought. If it would buy Talitha even one more second of life, he would give up his synagogue robes in a heartbeat. He would walk away from every privilege and prestige those robes afforded him. He would burn everything he owned and live the rest of his days a squalid beggar—if only he could have his Talitha back.

JESUS.

How wonderful it must be for a little girl to grow up with such a father, and I'm going to guess her mother was the same. How wonderful it must feel to be cherished and desired, valued and loved. How breathtaking to be wanted and nurtured, cared for and secured.

I would imagine that living day to day in such a cradle of parental devotion and fatherly affection would make for an extraordinary little girl. I don't mean extraordinary in achievement or smarts, although Talitha may well have been accomplished. And I don't mean extraordinaily witty or charming or any of those things that don't truly matter.

I mean extraordinary *in heart*. Extraordinary in comfort with herself and security of soul, unto fullness of life and freedom to be all the little girl that God created a girl to be. Oh for a home built in wholeness and safety! Oh for the treasure of a father's love!

I may be wrong, but that's how I picture little Talitha. I see a simply wonderful little girl with a happy heart, living her every day in a wonderland of delight. I see her rising every morning to the sound of birds chirping outside her window and the dawning sun warming her little room—this "Little Girl," who wakes every morning in the arms of safety and love.

And can't you just imagine her excitement when Daddy comes home from work each day? That's when the fun really begins! Talitha knows when it's nearly that time by the sun's hanging low on the horizon. When it isn't so cold, and even sometimes when it is, she waits for him outside in the courtyard. Some evenings she even waits outside the gate, which of course Mom doesn't like her to do. But sometimes Mom is too busy to see (please don't tell, okay?).

When Daddy rounds the corner, most often he has a package in his hand that's a little surprise just for her. He smiles such a big smile the moment he sees her face. Talitha *lives* to see that smile every day on her daddy's face. And every day, he does the exact same thing. He immediately stops and sets his package aside. He lifts his robe above his ankles and crouches down to the ground. Then he opens his arms wide—and Talitha runs into them as fast as her little feet will take her. She runs and runs and buries herself in the warmth of their waiting fold.

Talitha and her dad have been enjoying this ritual since before either of them can remember. Of course she's getting a little big these days, so it's harder for Dad to stay on his feet. Sometimes, lately, she almost knocks him over, so she needs to remember to slow down before she reaches him. But so far it's been okay.

And they just hug and kiss, right there in the street, right in front of everyone. There were a couple of times when it was raining, but even the rain didn't stop them. Talitha ran into her daddy's arms like she always did, and they just hugged and kissed.

JESUS.

Whatawful thing happened that stole this daddy's smile? What was it that stole the "little girl" from Talitha?

I'm going to guess that most people assume she became mortally ill, although the truth is that no one really knows. Scripture doesn't specifically say that Talitha got sick; it only says that she was dying (see Luke 8:42), and seven verses later, that she in fact died.

If I may step outside the lines of presumption, what if Talitha didn't get sick at all? Forgive me for the shock of saying this, but what if it was an act of violence that took her young life? What if some terrible someone hurt Talitha in some terrible way from which there was no recovering? It's so heartbreaking to consider, but the sin nature was as alive two thousand years ago as it is today, so I have to guess that those unconscionable things happened even then.

Violence—in whatever shape or form, big or small, once or more than once—can destroy all the "little girl" that is in a little girl. Even if Talitha hadn't died physically, how could a girl ever be the same? It's so painful to think about, that even as I write the words, I pray it wasn't so. Oh Father, have mercy.

See that you do not look down on one of these little ones.
For I tell you that their angels in heaven always see the
face of my Father in heaven.

—*Matthew 18:10*

JESUS.

Talitha's death could also have been a horrible accident. Things can happen, most especially in a first-century world where there were open wells and cooking fires and homes built of mud and straw. The roads turn to rivers every time there's a heavy rain, and the river tends to flood its banks. There's livestock to look after and ladders to climb that are made of tree limbs bound by homemade twine. The potential dangers of first-century life would have been all around Talitha.

Maybe one afternoon little Talitha looked to the sky and saw by the sun that it was almost time for her dad to come home. Maybe this particular afternoon, she got more excited than usual. Perhaps she'd missed him the day before because she'd played too long with her friend next door, and maybe Dad had teased her for that, and so she wasn't going to miss him this afternoon for anything.

Maybe it was one of those days when Mom wasn't looking, and so Talitha quietly lifted the latch on the gate. She stepped outside just as Daddy was coming around the bend. The moment he saw her, he smiled big and went into his crouch and opened his arms wide. And just as she always did, Talitha ran toward her dad as fast as she could. She ran and she ran and—

The boy on the donkey cart never saw her coming. His father wasn't at all like Talitha's dad. His father always got mad when the boy came home late, so the boy was rushing. He was so busy shouting at the donkey to go faster that he didn't see Talitha. Suddenly there she was, but it was too late to stop. And little Talitha lay still in the street.

Whatever it was that happened, one can only imagine that the joy in Jairus's home crumbled to the ground. Was it sickness that took Talitha? Was it violence or an accident? Did she lie suffering for a matter of moments, or for weeks or even years?

No one knows the answers to those questions, and it really doesn't matter. For where a little girl once lived and played and loved and dreamed—where her little girl's heart giggled with glee in the safety and warmth of her little girl's world—that little girl was now gone. Little Talitha was no more.

I don't know if anything aggrieves us more than the loss of a little girl. There's just something about those two words together, *little* and *girl*—the innocence, the defenselessness, the wholesomeness and purity. I would not be alone in saying that if there's one type of person that nothing bad should ever happen to, that type is little girls. And when a little girl passes on, no matter the circumstance or cause, it's as if it sort of stops the world.

At the same time, there is another kind of little-girl loss that doesn't stop the world. In fact it goes on every day, all around us, pretty much unnoticed and walked right by. It isn't literal, physical loss, but it is loss nonetheless. And though it receives little regard and takes on the appearance of normal life, it is a loss that is surely to be grieved.

I'm talking about when the little girl that lives inside of every . . . well . . . little girl, lives no more. I'm talking about those little-girl dreams and little-girl hopes, that little-girl innocence and joy and expectation. I'm talking about delight and excitement for life and living—that little-girl wonder that is so wonderfully and specifically *woman.*

I could be wrong, but I think that most every woman has little-girl dreams. By way of explanation, I think of my own niece and her zest for life and general sense of marvel about everything. She has this bedroom that her father affectionately calls The Pink Palace. It's my niece's "place." It's where she *goes*; where she's quiet and private.

It's where she lays her little head down at night with the moonlight beaming through her window. She lies nestled in the warmth of her pink comforter and looks up at the stars and listens to the crickets . . . and wonders what little girls wonder and dreams of all the marvelous possibilities that life can be.

Grown-up or not so grown-up, like my twelve-year-old

niece, I'm guessing that every woman has those kinds of little-girl dreams. It's just something that God puts inside a woman. It's an expectation, a hope. It's looking for the roses and finding the roses and smelling the roses, even where there are no roses. *It's the dream of a life that is so much more than life so regularly is.*

There's so much that comes against that "little girl." Dreams are fragile and easily bruised. Hurtful experiences and struggles come, and each one seems to whisper that the dreams can't ever be.

Sometimes life is exhausting, as a woman tries to get ahead in a world where soft and humble can mean last in line. Sometimes everything seems so hard, and a year turns into many years, and "it" never became what you dreamed it would be. Sometimes trust is so violently breached that it shatters every visage of romance and security a woman ever held in her heart . . . and the little girl who once giggled herself to sleep under the covers every night finds herself struggling to breathe.

Sometimes someone does something so dreadful to a woman that as much as she tries she can't seem to recover. And sometimes there's a horrible accident. Maybe she runs too fast on the wrong road and never reaches Daddy's arms . . . and the little girl inside of every woman's heart suddenly lies much too still. Her "talitha" is no more.

JESUS.

But then Jesus comes, and wonder awakes. He says, "Talitha, koum!" and hope and joy begin to breathe anew. The little girl rises afresh and free and is made alive all over again. Glory to the name of Jesus!

I imagine the moment two thousand years ago when Jesus first laid eyes on little Talitha. I imagine her family had "prepared" her somewhat, cleaning and dressing her, perhaps in her favorite robe. I imagine she would have been lying on her back with her little eyes closed. She would have been lying so very still.

It is breathtaking that Jesus sent the crowd outside. He was not a man who would use a little girl to show off his prowess and power. His God nature was the most sensitive reality in all the universe that day—just as it continues to be today. And so he approaches little Talitha with respect and care. He tiptoes toward her quietly and privately. This was to be Talitha's time entirely, and what lay in his heart for the fullness of her future was between just him and her.

I picture Jesus lowering his frame to the ground and kneeling by Talitha's side. He gazes at her little face for the longest time. I picture a tear forming in his eyes for all she had been through. This was never his Father's perfect plan. It is never his perfect desire that a little girl die.

I imagine Jesus brushing Talitha's check ever so lightly with the back of his hand. Even in death, her skin is so soft. Even with all the sad things that happened, she's still Talitha. She's still a little girl.

He draws very close. Oh so carefully, he slides one of his rugged palms beneath her sleeping hand. Perhaps he laces his fingers in between hers. Perhaps he holds both of her hands in his. He holds them as one would cradle a butterfly, being ever careful not to injure its wings.

I imagine Jesus looking at the shroud of her eyelids as if looking into her eyes. Then the words spill from his lips in a most tender and holy whisper, "Talitha, koum. I say to you, rise." It's the whisper of God to his sleeping beauty. *Your little-girl days are far from over. I've come to restore you, precious one. I've come to give you back your little-girl life.*

JESUS.

One can only imagine the joy that exploded in Jairus's household that wondrous day. One can only imagine little Talitha on Jesus' lap, giggling away as her family celebrated around them. I picture her chattering on about what she was now going to do and all the fun she was going to have and how absolutely wonderful her new life would be.

Late that night, as she lay curled in her little bed, nestled in the quiet security of her room, Talitha is so very sleepy from all the excitement of the day. Still, she struggles to keep herself awake so she can listen to the crickets and peek at the stars that smile down from the sky as they whisper through her window, "Welcome back, little one. Welcome home."

I wonder what Talitha dreamed that night. I wonder what little-girl hopes and plans danced in her little-girl's heart, afresh and new all over again. I wonder what expectations of all the wonders that tomorrows can bring tickled her thoughts and made her so excited that she could hardly wait for the morning to come—and the morning after, and the morning after . . .

Talitha was alive again. *The little girl lives.*

And Jesus turns from that first-century day to reach his heart toward yours. . . .

Yes, my precious one, the little girl lives. In me, by my hand, at the whisper of my voice, your Talitha lives.

I know the thieves that have tried to steal her from you, and I know the ways they've tried to crush her life. But precious one, I AM the Life, and I come today to restore all your life to you. I come to restore your abundance of life and to awaken your dreams and the delight and joyousness that have lain too still for far too long.

I know the hopes and future that I have for you, precious woman, and they are not for you to languish in your heart. They are not for you to suffer hardship or harm so that you lose your excitement and lightness of step.

My plans for you are good, little one. My plans for you are bountiful and aflame. They are for you to live in the fullness of your little-girl loveliness today and always—just as you grow more and more into the mature and capable woman that you already are.

And so I say to you, rise! I say, why all this commotion and wailing? The child is not dead but only asleep!

Hear my voice, precious woman, listen to my call. Talitha, koum! Little girl, arise!

I love you, Talitha. *I love you.*

JESUS.

Jesus said to her, "I am the resurrection and the life. He who believes in me will live, even though he dies."
—*John 11:25*

Who is this, robed in splendor, striding forward in the greatness of his strength? "It is I, speaking in righteousness, mighty to save."
—*Isaiah 63:1*

Away from me, all you who do evil, for the LORD has heard my weeping. The LORD has heard my cry for mercy.
—*Psalm 6:8–9*

I love you.
JESUS.

When Jesus rose early on the first day of the week,
he appeared first to Mary Magdalene,
out of whom he had driven seven demons.

—Mark 16:9

CHAPTER SIX

"Mary . . ."

I can't imagine that any book with a title like *Jesus, the Man Who Loved Women* could be complete without an exploration of Jesus and Mary Magdalene.

Mary Magdalene is easily among the most infamous women in the entire Bible, if not the most infamous of all. She is certainly the most renowned, not to mention controversial, woman Jesus is recorded to have known. I would even say she's downright mythical, if only in allusion to all the myth that has followed her.

So much has been written about Mary Magdalene that a writer like me, who hopes to bring something fresh to the discussion, can feel pretty intimidated. There are volumes of commentary, countless sermons and Bible-study curriculums, and several works of fiction all built upon her character. There are documentaries and Hollywood films, poems, songs, paintings, and sculptures.

Some characterize Mary Magdalene as being madly in love with Jesus—you know, the old "I Don't Know How to Love Him" story. And thanks to the novel *The Da Vinci Code*, scores believe she and Jesus settled down together and had a baby or two. The theory has intrigued so many that *Da Vinci Code* tours have become big business. "Ka-ching, Mary, ka-ching!"

The name of Mary Magdalene has also become synonymous with the word "prostitute." She is forever portrayed on film and stage and even preached about as a prostitute. I would guess that the vast majority of us, believers and nonbelievers alike, assume that's the way it was. She is solidly etched into our collective imagination as being a saucy, hard-edged vamp. *At least until she met Jesus.*

Truth be told, nowhere does Scripture say outright that Mary Magdalene was a prostitute. That is a fabrication that has no basis in documented fact. It's merely legend and tradition and a stunning testimony to the danger of not looking to the Word for truth. It's an example of presuming that just because someone said, wrote, or even preached it, it's fact. Literally for centuries, this precious woman has been tagged a prostitute, when it simply may not be true.

There is a school of thought that says Mary Magdalene may have been the woman who washed Jesus' feet with her tears (see Luke 7:36–50), and that's probably where the whole prostitute presumption started. Even in that story, however, the text does not say that this woman was a prostitute. The closest it comes is to say she "lived a sinful life." How fascinating it is that our minds would assume those words meant sex, when her sin could have been any sin—or even a mixture of many sins, which would make her . . . well . . . not so different from most all of us.

Then there's the woman who anointed Jesus with perfume at Bethany (see Matthew 26:6–13 and John 12:1–11). I have heard it taught that she was Mary Magdalene. Whether that is true or not is for the scholars to debate. All I know is that there is no mention of a prostitute in this story, either.

So may I shout in the face of centuries of unfounded presumption? Mary Magdalene was not necessarily a prostitute! Like any number of gospel women, she may have been a prostitute or she may not have been. We just plain don't know. Amen!

Based on what is clearly documented in Scripture, we only know one truth about Mary Magdalene before she met Jesus. We know only one most painful and heartrending truth: "When Jesus rose . . . , he appeared first to Mary Magdalene, *out of whom he had driven seven demons.*"

Mary Magdalene walked through life with seven demons. I don't know exactly what that means or what it looks like. I don't know if Mary was raving mad or if she appeared entirely normal and had just indulged so much in her life that she'd unwittingly "invited" these filthy things into her consciousness and way of thinking. I don't know any of this for sure, except that I couldn't imagine walking through life with even one demon.

Be self-controlled and alert.
Your enemy the devil prowls around like a roaring lion
looking for someone to devour.

—*1 Peter 5:8*

Dear God, have mercy.
JESUS.

I had an encounter, once, with a young woman who had three demons "in" her. I've actually had several such encounters as I serve in ministry, but this was so particularly eye-opening that I've often considered writing the story as its own book. She was standing outside a university church where I'd just finished speaking to the students.

It's too long a tale to tell in its entirety, but as I began to talk with her, the first thing that struck me was that she was filled with fear. As bizarre as this is going to sound, she was convinced that I would hurt her if I got too close. Even more, she was convinced that Jesus wanted to hurt her—even kill her. She was convinced of many things that simply were not true, and she was afraid of everything, really, and terribly confused.

While I was speaking with her, the scripture where Jesus asks a demon-possessed man his name popped into my head, and so I asked her name. Her answer will surely sit you back in your chair just as it spun me around that evening. Here was this nicely dressed young woman who looked perfectly normal, except for the fear in her eyes. She was this precious twenty-something girl who appeared no different from any other—and when I asked what her name was, she looked me square in the eye and said, "Black Death."

I asked her if she had any other names. "Black Snake," she replied, and then she added, "Deceit." At that point I didn't need a Ph.D. in theology to tell me I was dealing with something "other."

Jesus asked him, "What is your name?"
"My name is Legion," he replied, "for we are many."
—*Mark 5:9*

Her real name was Jenny, and if I may cut to the chase, the moment came when she voiced her desire for Jesus to come into her life and for these pests to go away. That act of her own will was pretty much the end of their story—though they didn't politely resign and go quietly. One by one, they did everything they could to deceive her into thinking she would die without them.

He was a murderer from the beginning,
not holding to the truth, for there is no truth in him.
When he lies, he speaks his native language,
for he is a liar and the father of lies.
—*John 8:44*

As Jenny was telling Black Death to go, it was as if she were choking. I assured her that she wasn't really choking, but that her intruder was lying to her; as she pressed through, the sensation of choking stopped. With Black Snake, it was as if her heart were going to explode. Deceit made her think her head was exploding. She pressed through each deception, and one by one, they disappeared from her mind and heart. They each disappeared "just like that."

I would add one more detail that is something of an aside, but it is the most important detail of all. Jenny told me about terrible things she had done in her life—truly unmentionable horrors. I held as cool a face as possible and just kept saying over and over, "He loves you, Jenny. He forgives you, and he loves you."

That was when the bad guys *really* packed their bags. You should have seen them melt in the power of that most awesome truth. I could see it in Jenny's countenance, which completely changed. Her eyes welled with huge tears, and her whole body went weak as the pureness of God's heart embraced her understanding.

In the face of Jesus' love and forgiveness, the bad guys were powerless to do what was obviously the only thing they could do—*deceive her*. They were powerless to hold her mind and heart as that mighty reality took root in Jenny's precious soul. Glory to the name of Jesus!

From start to finish that night, I was with Jenny for about three hours. There was no shouting at Jenny or banging on her head or any of that showy stuff you sometimes see on television or wherever. Calmly, we talked together. Calmly, we talked of Jesus. And Jenny walked away a demon-free, born-again, happy and precious girl.

JESUS.

Why do I tell this story? Because as I experienced those demons that night, the only thing they could do to Jenny was deceive her. They lied and lied to her. Who knows for how many years and how deeply? They even tried to lie to me, as well, that night. And my experience has been exactly the same in other encounters. They just lie—period. It is so broad-brush that I would even suggest that lying is the only thing they *can* do. I would suggest that their entire "power," if you can call it that, is in their capacity to deceive.

Jenny is free today. She's *free*. Glory to the name of Jesus!

Demons do one thing in a woman's life: they try to convince her of things that aren't true. They tell a woman she isn't what she is. They tell her she is what she isn't. They do everything they can to convince her that she's less than who God made her to be.

Their hope is to tear a woman down and tear others down with her, and so they mask and mar a woman's beauty in truth. They stir the pot of uncertainty. They whisper lies in the ears of her soul—lies that contradict the confidence and strength and loveliness that God has planted in every woman's soul. They distract and distort and deceive, in an unceasing bid for the most precious places of a woman's heart.

And they lie through the most ordinary and everyday means,

through which they tiptoe undercover and unnoticed. Sometimes they lie through a billboard or a fashion magazine, whispering, "You're not enough." Sometimes it's through a television show about the privileged, rich, and famous. They lie through the not-so-funny jabs that so often spill from loved ones' mouths. They even lie through preachers who don't accurately teach.

They lie through fathers and mothers who weren't the fathers or mothers God wanted them to be. They lie through school kids who can be so cruel and through neighbors who always seem to have better. They lie through failures that make a woman feel . . . well . . . like a failure. They lie through relationships that didn't work out.

They trick a woman through feelings, which can change like the wind. They hook into impatience, rejection, and want. They deceive through flattery and well-intended advice. They belittle a woman, using another woman's figure, sense of style, or success.

Their whisper surely follows every sin and mistake: *And you actually believe God still loves you?* When loneliness comes, they shout: *You'll always be by yourself. No one wants you.* Sometimes they seem to dance inside our thoughts: *You're nothing. You're nobody. You'd better move fast and take what you can get.*

I could fill volumes with their lies and the pathways that their lies follow, but I'm going to guess that the point is made. And with every lie's success, big or small—at every point where a woman embraces the lie—that woman's heart is injured. Her womanhood is harmed. Her fullness of life is chipped away.

JESUS.

Two thousand years ago, for whatever reason, Mary Magdalene had believed too many lies. Who knows why? Maybe gaping holes of vulnerability were opened in her childhood by an upbringing that was filled with pain. Perhaps the deceptions began to fill her infant mind before she could even form a conscious thought. Perhaps deep in the womb, she heard devastating words like, "I don't want another child." "Abort the stupid thing!" "Why is this happening to me?"

Maybe as a small girl her brother's friend snuck into her room and did something so terrible that it left her with a gash through which the lies poured in. Maybe Dad died and left her alone, and there was no one around to tell her what was true. Or perhaps— God forbid—he just plain left her.

It's possible that some other little boy or girl taught Mary something that seemed kind of fun but seemed a little wrong too. But a lot of kids were doing it, so why not? Or as a young woman there was something inside Mary that made her want to explore—made her try a little of this and some of that. Maybe some man stepped on her heart so cruelly that she turned her back on true love and ran into the hell of false love.

Whatever Mary's point or points of vulnerability were over many years, no doubt, one day she believed a lie. Then she believed another lie and another. She made choices based on those lies—choices that drove her deeper into lies and made her run even faster toward the lies and the deceptively warm company that lies often portray.

What Mary Magdalene didn't know was that the lies and the liars behind them were murderers "from the beginning." Murder was their agenda from day one. Their hope was to kill her—to kill her with lies.

Oh, they couldn't outright physically murder her. If they had that kind of power and free rein, then not a one of us would be breathing today. At the same time, as Mary embraced one lie upon another, the lies could collectively kill "her." Slowly but surely they could kill her woman's heart. They could kill her womanly confidence and potential and her woman's dreams.

They could choke away her wholeness of life and tear down her womanly worth. They could sling so much denigration at her self-respect and value that she became convinced she was little more than nothing. They could beat down her dignity until her esteem as a woman—the esteem that filled her with hope and allowed her to hold her head high in God's wondrous image— struggled to breathe . . . or simply was no more.

Mary Magdalene had seven demons. Why or how or what they looked like we don't know. But in the midst of it all and as a result of them all, I picture Mary walking through her days with her head hanging low. I picture her fearful and confused and always looking back on her life, asking why did this happen? and, how come that happened? I imagine her feeling like a nobody, moving through her daily tasks—the washing, the well, the work in the field—with her eyes to the ground, avoiding the eyes of women who always seemed to be "more."

Mary has grown so weary of hearing other people's good stories and having none of her own that she would sooner be by herself. So as much as possible she keeps to herself. It's easier that way, and besides, no one really seems to notice her.

Then there was that day in the marketplace when Mary stood in the shadows by the butcher's stall and watched that woman who has such nice kids and a wonderful husband. She always dresses beautifully and smiles so pretty. Everyone likes her so much, and Mary remembers how, when the two of them were little girls growing up, she always seemed to do everything right. Even then people liked her. Even then she seemed to be someone special.

Yes, I picture Mary as tired inside and feeling so very small. I picture her a little unkempt—after all, what did it matter? I imagine her feeling dirty, even, and somehow lesser for all the lies and the hurting roads she'd traveled at the lies' urgings.

I imagine Mary's biggest laugh in life was to think she could ever be like that woman in the marketplace. I picture her alone inside herself, feeling forgotten and left out . . . until that miracle day when she looked up from the lies and into the eyes of living Truth—that day when she looked into the eyes of Jesus.

The thief comes only to steal and kill and destroy;
I have come that they may have life,
and have it to the full.
—John 10:10

How does a woman go from being one of the most confused and forgotten to one of the most privileged and celebrated women in human history? How does she go from walking in the shadows to walking with Jesus and standing in the place of ultimate honor— by his mother's side—at the foot of his cross? How does a woman who most everyone passed by, and who'd made so many mistakes and had long given up on dignity and worth, become the first person to whom Jesus revealed himself after he rose from the dead?

It is a mind-bending reality to consider that Jesus would choose Mary Magdalene for these positions of such monumental and timeless tribute. There were daughters of kings and accomplished women all around him. There were educated women with great skills and wisdom. He could have chosen a woman of stellar reputation or a woman like the one Mary watched from the shadows in the market that day, who did everything right her entire life. Jesus could have chosen any one of them at any time—*but, instead, he chose Mary.*

He chose a woman who had nothing to offer except the shattered pieces of her broken life. He chose a woman who meant little to the world and probably even less to herself. He chose a sinner besieged by lies and the liars who carry them. He chose a woman who, one embraced lie at a time, had all but thrown her life away.

I wonder what it was like for Mary that very first time she stood face to face with Jesus. Perhaps she was passing through the center of her village on the way home from a long, hard day and just happened to turn—and there he stood, looking right at her. I imagine Mary's mind racing—she knew who Jesus was and the wonders that people said he did. She'd heard all the talk about him in the streets. Surely he couldn't be looking at *her*. But, yes, he was looking at her. This man whom everyone in the ancient world was looking at was looking only at her.

So, slowly, she raises her countenance. She dares to return his holy gaze. She musters every tattered and battered shred of what's left of her courage and looks back into his eyes.

And suddenly, her everything else ceased to matter. Her past no longer mattered. Her mistakes no longer mattered. It didn't matter what people thought of her or, even more, what she thought of herself. Even that woman in the marketplace whom Mary envied didn't matter. Suddenly all that mattered was in this man's eyes. All that mattered was *Jesus*.

I imagine Mary saw her future in Jesus' eyes that day. I imagine she saw in them the woman she truly was, as opposed to the woman the lies had convinced her to be. I imagine it was something akin to the story of Aldonza and Don Quixote in *Man of La Mancha*. Without a word his eyes whispered, *I know who you've come to believe you are, precious one, and it is all untrue. What you see in my eyes is who you really are—a princess, a queen, a treasure to be honored and esteemed.*

I love you, precious woman. And oh, the plans I have for you! My name is Jesus, and I love you.

And in the simplicity of his gaze, all the lies were laid bare. In the prowess of his presence, the liars turned to flee. The balm of his truth poured into the woundedness they left behind, and the door was opened for Mary to begin afresh. Mary was now free to adorn herself in womanhood anew, as her heart filled with an understanding of the woman Jesus had created her to be.

You will know the truth, and the truth will set you free.
—John 8:32

JESUS.

You know, the details of what actually took place during that first encounter are not recorded in the Gospels. But I wonder if, in the middle of that first gaze, Jesus didn't smile one of those Jesus smiles and reach out his hand and call her name—*Mary.*

The reason I wonder that is because of what happened between Jesus and Mary Magdalene at the tomb, when he was arisen from the dead. She thought he was the gardener that morning. He stood before her plain as day. He even spoke to her, and still she didn't know it was him. But then Jesus called her name—"Mary"—and immediately she knew. Oh how she must have thrown herself into Jesus' arms. Oh how she must have cried and cried.

> *Jesus said to her, "Mary."*
> *She turned toward him and*
> *cried out in Aramaic, "Rabboni!" (which means Teacher).*
> —*John 20:16*

I've heard several explanations concerning that mystery encounter, most of which lean toward the supernatural. But none of them ever rang to me as more than someone's best guess, and the reality is that no one really knows for sure. So I can't help but wonder if the truth of the matter isn't something more human— something real and down-to-earth, something so "Jesus," if you will, and downright lovely.

I wonder if he called her name that morning in a special way that had developed along with their friendship. I have to guess that Jesus developed wonderful friendships with all the men and women who walked with him and with whom he worked so closely during his three years of ministry.

I wonder if the way he said "Mary" wasn't just one of those little "things" friends have with friends that are a kind of private communication. Maybe it was a certain tone in his voice that was there that very first day they met, and it just stuck with them. Maybe from then on, every time Mary felt down on herself or felt like giving up, Jesus would look at her say, "Mary," and she would know what he meant, and nothing more needed to be said.

Yes, I wonder if it didn't begin that very first day when Jesus reached one of his strong carpenter hands toward her and smiled from here to . . . well . . . eternity. Mary would have been so frightened to be singled out that day, so confused and unsure. But then Jesus speaks her name.

How does he know my name? At first that scares her even more, but at the same time it somehow calms her heart. It's in the timbre of his voice. It's in his quality of truthfulness. She believes this man—and so she offers her hand. With the care and respect due a lady of honor, he receives it into both of his.

JESUS.

In the days and perhaps even years that followed that first meeting of Jesus and Mary, he would wash her free of all the lies that had besieged her, and he would rewrite her entire destiny. He would take her from meaning so little to herself and most everyone else and escort her into the most meaningful events in universal history. Just as he may have spoken her name that day for the very first time, he would lift her name into the preeminence of his eternal, living Word and place it alongside the names of queens and presidents in the annals of world history.

Jesus loved Mary, pure and simple. He reached into her life and restored her dignity and value. He restored her womanly hope. He cherished and respected her just the way she was—with seven demons and maybe as a prostitute (or maybe not)—and in the safety of his acceptance, Mary Magdalene became all the woman he'd birthed her to be . . .

And I love you, too, my precious one. Do you not hear me calling your name as well? I esteem you. I value you. I honor you.

Reach for my hand that I may lift you, too. Reach for my hand that I may lift you from wherever you are and into the place you've always dreamed of.

Turn away from the lies that devalue—and turn to me. They are only lies, my precious one. They have no power. I alone AM *power.*

Feel my gentle hand beneath your chin and raise your eyes to meet mine. See in my eyes who you really *are. That's right, my precious one—who you really are in me.*

I love you, I love you.

JESUS.

Daughters of kings are among your honored women; at your right hand is the royal bride in gold of Ophir.
—*Psalm 45:9*

I love you.
JESUS.

Jesus sat down opposite the place where
the offerings were put and watched the crowd
putting their money into the temple treasury.
Many rich people threw in large amounts.
But a poor widow came and put in two very small
copper coins, worth only a fraction of a penny.
Calling his disciples to him, Jesus said,
"I tell you the truth, this poor widow has
put more into the treasury than all the others.
They all gave out of their wealth; but she,
out of her poverty, put in everything—
all she had to live on."

—Mark 12:41–44

"More Than All the Others"

Patiently she stood at the offering bin waiting her turn. Quietly Jesus watched as she waited. He watched as she pulled a folded piece of cloth from her waistband and removed two tiny coins. He watched as she drew her hand up into her sleeve to hide them. She was hoping no one would see. But Jesus did see. And tears of love filled his eyes. . . .

I have often thought that we live in a world where the wrong people receive the greatest honor and all the accolades. The wrong kinds of achievements arrest our attention, while the true heroes of life—the truly brave and courageous and driven and accomplished—rarely, if ever, receive even a nod.

I don't mean to discount men and women who have made great contributions to our world, be it in business or politics or humanitarian effort. I don't mean to say there is nothing to admire in an accomplished sports figure, artist, or intellectual. And in our Christian world, there are certainly people who have done marvelous works on behalf of God's kingdom. If I were a man who wore a hat, I'd tip my hat to them all.

In my own life, I had a "season" of applause. Those of you who are familiar with my past work will know that as an actor I once played the role of Jesus in a film that took many corners of the world by storm. That experience is what opened my eyes to the humanity and "reality" of Jesus, to the wonder of his heart and the breath-stealing extent of his love. That role is what has propelled my writing, and every book I've written since then has been about Jesus.

Another result of that role is that I found myself sharing Jesus from the platforms of some of America's and the world's largest churches. I found myself standing before university audiences, banquets, conventions, and conferences. I found myself on the covers of Christian magazines and on television talk shows and sharing the stage with the likes of Michael W. Smith in front of thousands.

Letters poured in from all over the world, each one describing how God touched a life through the film, a book, or a speaking engagement. Every place I spoke, there was standing room only. People lined up afterward to shake my hand or share their testimony.

I received phone calls and emails from Christian leaders saying things like "anointed of God" and "part of God's plan to return his people's focus to Jesus." My pastor at the time, Jack Hayford, invited me to his home. On the humorous side, every time I went to church, women were suddenly smiling and saying hello. They were the same women who had walked by me for years without so much as a glance.

It's not like that for me today, although my life is still very public, and the testimonies (praise God!) continue to flow. Those of you who are familiar with me know that my life has now settled down to nuts-and-bolts ministry. And by the way, I hardly ever get those smiles from the girls at church anymore. Oh well, so much for "perks."

The reason I share that story is to say that I've been on that side of the fence, so to speak, and I can tell you from experience that it's very easy to be "great" when everyone is telling you you're great. It's easy to keep going when everyone is cheering you on. It's easy to care when they pat you on the back. It's easy to give when there is so much return. It's easy to sacrifice when everyone knows.

At the same time, there are many all around us, every day, whose giving goes pretty much unnoticed, let alone receives an accolade. Still they keep giving and caring. They bow their pride and put their own wants and needs on the shelf. Day upon day, they quietly go about the business of sacrifice and responsibility, faithfulness and servanthood. They quietly live as champions to an audience of few to none.

These are the true heroes and heroines. They are the ones who deserve the honor. These are the men and women who should be on the covers of our (Christian) magazines. These are the men and women we should be admiring and clamoring to see.

At the same time, these heroes are not lost on Jesus. As the saying goes, "His eye is on the sparrow." It's a saying based on Matthew 10:29–30. "Are not two sparrows sold for a penny? Yet not one of them will fall to the ground apart from the will of your Father. And even the very hairs of your head are all numbered." The saying communicates that while our human eyes are on the eagles and swans and peacocks of this life, his divine eyes are on . . . well . . . maybe you.

Oh, little sparrow who reads these words—who works so hard and is so faithful and just gives and gives—*his eyes are on you.* When he smiles from his throne, his smile is for you. When he applauds from his throne, his applause is unto you. He loves you, little sparrow. *He loves you.*

> *He views the ends of the earth*
> *and sees everything under the heavens.*
> —*Job 28:24*

JESUS.

They were tense times for Jesus as he sat watching the old widow in the temple courtyard that day. He was very near the cross, and the heat of persecution and conflict was at its most sizzling. Daily he taught, and daily he was attacked. The religious powers were scrambling to destroy him any way they could, and the plotting behind his back was at fever pitch.

Every day he was teaching at the temple.
But the chief priests, the teachers of the law
and the leaders among the people were trying to kill him.
—*Luke 19:47*

Over and over Jesus was challenged, confronted, insulted, and defied. He was called a demon and who knows what ugly else. He was made to defend his position and was backed into corners of rock-and-a-hard-spot debate.

"Teacher, should we pay taxes?"

"If a woman marries seven brothers, whose wife is she?"

"How can you lawfully heal on the Sabbath?"

"By what authority do you do these things?"

The temple guards flanked his every move, at the ready to take him in. There were near escapes from being stoned. There were mobs gone wild and fighting among the people and hiding to save his life—until the appointed time.

The Pharisees went out
and plotted how they might kill Jesus.
Aware of this, Jesus withdrew from that place.
—*Matthew 12:14–15*

JESUS.

We tend to have a "religious" sense of Jesus floating stoically through all these assaults. We have seen films and paintings that show him standing tall through them all, meeting every Pharisaical chal-lenge with calmly spoken, higher wisdom. Jesus opens his mouth, and a hush falls over the crowd. Entirely trumped, his attackers cower in shame and turn away with their tails tucked beneath their robes.

It is true about the higher wisdom and that his answers stumped them all. At the same time, we are greatly deceived if we forget that Jesus was a man. He was a man with a human heart filled with human feelings. As much as he was simultaneously God, he took no divine advantage over you and me.

He would have felt fatigue and disappointment. He would have felt the sting of insult and assault. He would have felt what anyone would feel who was only trying to save and heal and care—who was daily giving his life away—and got laughed at and attacked and spit upon in return.

As a result, I picture Jesus in those "final" temple days being so very tired. I picture him in a place of such human need for someone to somehow show him that his sweat and tears haven't been shed for naught. As it is, the crowds come and go. They listen to his words and then whisper about him as if he doesn't know.

They argue about him and decide for or against him. They do it day upon day—and in his heart, he knows that the hour will soon come when they'll forget all of his healing and saving and raising from the dead, and cry out to Pilate for his blood.

And so he seats himself in a moment of private reprieve. He takes a moment to stop and breathe. Maybe he takes a rag and soaks it in water, then presses its coolness against his face. Perhaps he reaches into a satchel and draws out a piece of fruit, quietly enjoying a little something to eat—a little something to build up his strength for the next round of confrontation.

Jesus was as driven a man as there ever has been in history, but on this day there's a part of him that's just *so* tired. He's worked hard to reach "his babies," and he sits, grieving in his heart as they walk about him, so fascinated by the temple's gold, marble, and other trappings that don't really count. It all just hits him more than it usually does, and in his heart he feels *tired*.

He hears a murmur of excitement and turns his eyes toward the offering bins. People swarm around a nicely dressed man and his nicely dressed wife as they receive hugs from the priests and pats on the back and probably invitations to dinner. Everyone is abuzz over the amount of money they just dropped into the bins. Everyone is so impressed.

Oh how Jesus has spoken over and over that such things—the things of wealth and worldly success—should not be what captures their attention. They nod their heads and shout, "Hallelujah!," but still their attention is captured. Jesus glances toward his disciples, and he can see that even some of them are intrigued.

Then something captures *his* attention. It's the "poor widow," waiting patiently for all the hoopla to subside. Perhaps Jesus recognizes her face. Yes, it was in this very courtyard that she sat quietly one day, listening to him teach while others threw insults and called him a demon.

He remembers noticing her clothes and thinking, *She must have so little.* But most of all he remembers the look that was in her eyes. He could see that she understood his every word—*in her heart* she understood—and that she so loved his Father. And he remembers how big that made him smile inside, and how it gave him the strength to keep going.

Now she stands at the offering bin privately waiting while everyone continues to crowd around that nice-looking couple. She overhears one of the priests saying how much they gave. It's more money than the widow has known in many years. She opens her palm and looks at her two tiny coins. She closes her palm and hides them even more.

The crowd finally moves on, and she's left all alone. She looks left and right, then closes her eyes and lowers her head. Shyly she lifts her hands to her waist. Her lips begin to move in silent prayer. Jesus watches—*Jesus hears*—as her lips move in silent prayer.

She steps up and goes to her tiptoes to reach the lip of the bin. She reaches as high as her reach can take her. She opens her fingers, the coins drop in—and Jesus' eyes fill with tears.

> *I tell you the truth, this poor widow has put more*
> *into the treasury than all the others.*
> —*Mark 12:43*

JESUS.

I think a woman ministers to Jesus when she quietly gives. I'm not speaking so much about financial giving, like this precious woman, or volunteering at church or mission work or the like. Those things are wonderful in their own right, and there's no doubt they touch his heart as well.

What I'm talking about, though, is a woman who quietly gives in her daily living. She gives of herself in day-to-day faithfulness. She gives of herself in responsibility. She makes the giving choices in her everyday life—choices that honor her commitments and honor him.

There's no shouting or fanfare. No one applauds or cheers this woman on. No one even recognizes her as doing anything extraordinary, as it all appears so "normal life." She's just a woman quietly toughing it out, even though it hurts sometimes. She's a woman putting her own needs on the shelf over and over, finding strength even when she has none, and going the distance though her heart is sometimes weary.

As a wife, she gives to her husband. As a mother, she gives to her children. As a wife or a mother, or none of the above, she works at her job "as unto him." She pays her bills and plays it straight and does what she has to do to make ends meet. She sets her alarm early to spend time in prayer and goes to bed late because things need to be done.

She says no when she wants to say yes and always seems to say yes when she'd rather say no. She gives to her mother and to her father—she would never abandon them. She visits Aunt Sally, who is battling cancer, even though Aunt Sally was always so mean. She puts fresh flowers on Granny's grave because everyone else has pretty much forgotten.

As an unmarried woman, she says no to that guy who is so very attractive but doesn't yet know Jesus. She lives within her means and always takes the time when her friends who are struggling need to talk. She takes care of the nephews and takes Mom out on Sundays, and she invites that coworker who's going through divorce for coffee. Sometimes she just sits home on Saturday night because she knows that's where Jesus wants her to be. She sits home, and he sees. He smiles, and he sees.

Then there are the single moms. I think of so many mothers who have to be strong and go it alone. They deny themselves and shoulder their responsibilities like champions. They keep giving to their kids though Daddy is gone, and it gets hard sometimes. The apartment is too small, but "we'll make it somehow," and they just keep giving of themselves.

Mistakes are made, of course, and sometimes they're big mistakes. But at the end of the day, Mom is there. At the end of the day, Mom is Dad too. And when the lights go out at night, the little ones go to sleep knowing that Mom will never leave them no matter who else has—*and Jesus smiles*. Oh how he smiles. Single mom, Jesus sees, and Jesus smiles.

Whoever welcomes a little child like this
in my name welcomes me.
—*Matthew 18:5*

JESUS.

I have often wondered if this widow whom Jesus watched that long-ago day might have been a single mother. Traditionally we picture her as an elderly woman, which may well have been the case, but we really don't know. She could have actually been young. She may have even been very young.

Who knows if she didn't marry and get pregnant and was excited about her family's future, but then almost immediately something terrible happened to her husband? Oh Father, have mercy.

She could have been . . . well . . . like Jesus' own mother when he was just a boy. After all, Joseph is never again mentioned in the Gospels after Jesus is twelve years old. Scripture gives us no documented reason for that, but most scholars guess he died. If, indeed, that was the case, Mary would have been a single mom with small children. Mary, too, would have been a "poor widow."

Yes, I wonder if, as Jesus watched this precious woman put her tiny coins into the offering bin, he thought of his own mother.

Maybe, as a boy, there were times when he'd stood in that exact same spot and held his mother's hand as she dropped her offering into the bin. Maybe there were times when all Mary had to give were "two very small copper coins, worth only a fraction of a penny." Who knows? Maybe Jesus had seen his own mother's embarrassment in the shadow of the well-heeled and congratulated. If that poor widow truly was a mother with child, maybe that child "was" him.

As Jesus watched, perhaps he remembered all the nights when his mom cried herself to sleep. Perhaps he recalled the way she regularly went without so her children might have nice clothes. Or maybe he thought about the sacrifices his mother made so that, no matter what, they always had something to give at the temple.

He remembered the times when he wasn't feeling well and his mother would stay up with him all night, even though she wasn't feeling well either. He remembered the jobs she did on the side for the neighbors, hauling their water and chopping their wood. He remembered the men whom she said no to, because they wouldn't have cared for his brothers and sisters and him.

Jesus sat quietly watching this precious woman who was "going it" alone. He remembered his own mother going it alone. He watched and remembered and smiled through the tears that filled his eyes all the more.

Jesus loved that poor widow. She was just like his mother—the stuff of which his kingdom was made. She was one of "the last" whom he couldn't wait to make first. She was one of the forgotten who are forever held in the deep of his Father's heart.

> *But many who are first will be last,*
> *and many who are last will be first.*
> —*Matthew 19:30*

JESUS.

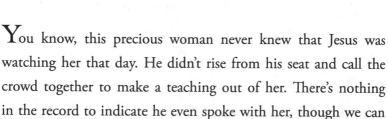

You know, this precious woman never knew that Jesus was watching her that day. He didn't rise from his seat and call the crowd together to make a teaching out of her. There's nothing in the record to indicate he even spoke with her, though we can pretty well guess what gracious words he would have shared.

She just quietly put her coins in the bin and then, probably just as quietly, walked away. She had no idea she'd captured the attention of the Word Became Flesh. She had no idea that the eyes of the living God were upon her. She had no idea he'd heard her prayers. Indeed, he'd watched her prayers and seen her prayers— and felt them so deeply that he cried.

I imagine that, unsuspecting, she put her head down and shuffled toward whatever it was that she called home. I imagine her thinking, *There goes dinner tonight,* and maybe even chuckling at herself for giving it all away. And I imagine Jesus' eyes following and never leaving her as she melted into the crowd and disappeared from view.

She was just an everyday woman. She was a woman who gives. She was a woman, perhaps, not so different from you—and she brought so much joy to Jesus. Without even knowing, she refreshed his soul and profoundly touched his heart. Her actions silently whispered, "Keep going, Jesus," and gave him strength to press through, no matter what hardships were to come.

She didn't know he was watching, and she didn't know he was God. She just gave of herself as a woman gives of herself—and she gave herself to God.

I can only imagine the tenderness that must have overtaken Jesus' thoughts toward that woman that day. I can only imagine the affections that inspired his flow of holy tears. They are, no doubt, the same affections that rise in his heart toward you, precious woman, today . . .

> *You are not lost on me, my precious one. Do not think for one second that you are forgotten. Though the world may forsake you, I never will. Though the world may pass you by, I AM yours always.*
>
> *My eyes are upon you every step of your way, and my smile is because of you. Your ways—your heart and care and*

all those little things you think are insignificant—are always in my sight. I don't miss even one. I record them all, and I hold them deeply in my heart. Indeed, I hold you in my heart.

You've worked so hard and given so much. You are quietly faithful. You've cared and sacrificed and put yourself last. You've given without thought of return.

I know there were times when you could have withheld. I remember the times when you wondered, Why am I doing this? *I know that you sometimes felt so very alone, because as much as you gave, nobody seemed to care, and you even began to wonder if I wasn't one of them.*

Oh precious one, I see and I know. I know you've shed tears in the night and that many a night you cried yourself to sleep. I know that sometimes it seems I've given you little. I know that it often feels as if every parade of life passes you by.

My precious woman, don't ever be deceived by the bang and clatter of human notice or enticed by the things that draw attention. Hear the bigness of my voice when I tell you they mean nothing. *I* AM *never where the crowd is, precious one. My eye is always on the sparrow. And remember— sooner or later, the one chased by the crowd today is forgotten by the crowd tomorrow.*

Let them exalt each other and tell themselves how wonderful they are. Let them boast of how I've blessed them and how they're always getting ahead. Let them walk proudly in those illusions—and all the while, you just keep being who you are. *Just keep doing as you do. Just keep giving as you give. Keep caring and being faithful in all those tiny ways you think no one ever sees*—but I do.

I have seen, oh, precious one. I have watched you. And all of heaven stands to their feet and applauds. My Father is pleased, as am I, and together we say, "Well done."

Did you hear those words, precious woman? Did they land in your heart? "Well done, good and faithful woman." Well done.

Your "two copper coins" are as billions of dollars. Your fraction of a penny overwhelms me. You bless me, pure and simple. And of all who clamor about me, it is you who has my gaze. Of all who think I AM so pleased, it is you who touches my heart.

I love you, precious woman. I love you.

JESUS.

As he was leaving the temple, one of his disciples said to him, "Look, Teacher! What massive stones! What magnificent buildings!"
"Do you see all these great buildings?" replied Jesus.
"Not one stone here will be left on another; every one will be thrown down."
—Mark 13:1–2

Where can I go from your Spirit?
Where can I flee from your presence?
If I go up to the heavens, you are there;
if I make my bed in the depths, you are there.
If I rise on the wings of the dawn,
if I settle on the far side of the sea,
even there your hand will guide me,
your right hand will hold me fast.
—Psalm 139:7–10

I love you.
JESUS.

Jacob's well was there, and Jesus,
tired as he was from the journey, sat down by the well.
It was about the sixth hour.
When a Samaritan woman came to draw water,
Jesus said to her, "Will you give me a drink?"

—*John 4:6–7*

"I Who Speak to You Am He"

The story of the Samaritan woman, or as she is more popularly known, "the woman at the well," is as iconic a gospel story as there is. At the same time, at least in my mind, it is also one of the most difficult to understand or even accept as real when held up to the norms of human interaction and the absolute love, care, and gentleness of Jesus toward hurting people.

Don't get me wrong. I'm not suggesting the encounter never happened or that the apostle John didn't document it accurately. It's just that so much of what is spoken between Jesus and this woman doesn't quite make sense for two people who have never before met. In addition, there is much that makes Jesus appear insensitive at the least, and sometimes even rude.

For starters, he sits and watches as she balances pots and water jars and who knows what other heavy things. And not only does Jesus not offer to help, but he actually gives her more work to do. It was during "the sixth hour," which was in the heat of the afternoon. She'd just carried all this load up from the village. There she is, sweating in the sun, bent over the well, hauling up buckets of water—and he asks her to give him a drink. He doesn't even extend the courtesy of introducing himself first.

Put yourself in that woman's shoes (or sandals as the case may be). You're working hard, and some stranger who's sitting there doing nothing asks, "Will you give me a drink?" All religiosity aside, I can guess that most women would tell a guy like that to get his own drink. Most women would think he was the most arrogant man they'd ever met, and justifiably so. Forgive me for saying this, but if it wasn't Jesus and it wasn't in the pages of the gospel, we would be appalled at a man behaving in such a manner.

To make things worse, as their exchange continues, Jesus seemingly talks in "riddles" all throughout. He never once answers this woman's questions outright. Forgive me again, but is there anything more irritating?

The Samaritan woman said to him,
"You are a Jew and I am a Samaritan woman.
How can you ask me for a drink?"
(For Jews do not associate with Samaritans.)
Jesus answered her, "If you knew the gift of God
and who it is that asks you for a drink, you would have
asked him and he would have given you living water."
—John 4:9–10

Shaking free of the hindsight and spiritual eyes through which you and I understand what Jesus was saying that day, again, put yourself in the Samaritan woman's shoes. Can you imagine hearing words like that—from a grown man sitting by a well while every other respectable man is out working? What would you think? *Living water? Like, what is that supposed to mean?*

Then out of nowhere Jesus blurts, "Go, call your husband and come back" (John 4:16). You would think she would have been shocked that a stranger could be so familiar. It makes no human sense (to me anyway) that she didn't just tell him to go take a hike.

You have to understand that you and I read this woman's story in the larger picture of God's plan for salvation and the principles he's trying to teach us through it. We know that the man she was talking with was the Son of the living God and, in that framework, everything he says makes sense. It makes *spiritual* sense. It's all perfectly understandable and, because it's Jesus speaking, perfectly wonderful and acceptable.

On that blistering hot afternoon, however, there was no spiritual hindsight. When the Samaritan woman heard, "Will you give me a drink?" and turned to look, the man she saw appeared to be no different from any other man. There was nothing about him that said, "Son of God." On the surface and to the human eye, there was nothing about him that even said, "Special."

He grew up before him like a tender shoot,
and like a root out of dry ground.
He had no beauty or majesty to attract us to him,
nothing in his appearance that we should desire him.
—*Isaiah 53:2*

Given the undeniable truth of Isaiah's words, it seems almost bizarre that this woman didn't, at least, just ignore Jesus. It's baffling that she even engaged him. And beyond that, she carried on as if nothing was at all unusual.

"I have no husband," she replied.
Jesus said to her, "You are right when you say you have
no husband. The fact is, you have had five husbands, and
the man you now have is not your husband. What you
have just said is quite true."
—*John 4:17–18*

JESUS.

I've heard several explanations of those mysteries above. I've heard it said that it was normal within the culture for a man to ask a woman for a drink, as Jesus did. I've also heard it taught that

Jesus' words pierced her heart so deeply that she was convicted and enthralled.

Those explanations notwithstanding, the bottom line is actually much more obvious, simple, and practical: John's account is not necessarily the entire story. After all, John wasn't even there. The apostles had gone into town to buy food (see John 4:8). There may have been many words exchanged between Jesus and this precious woman that simply didn't get recorded.

More significant, every detail John recorded in his every gospel story was recorded unto one very specific purpose:

> *These are written that you may believe*
> *that Jesus is the Christ, the Son of God,*
> *and that by believing you may have life in his name.*
> —John 20:31

Preceding that verse John writes that "Jesus did many other miraculous signs." So in John's own words, there was a great deal he didn't record, simply because it didn't serve his gospel's purpose.

There is more. As it is with every story in John's Gospel, two things are going on simultaneously. There is the simple human interaction that actually, historically happened. Every detail we read is real. Then there is the big picture—may I say, a "prophetic" picture—that John wants us to see. Jesus wants us to see it as well; in fact, in the moment and on the day, he intentionally purposed it.

In other words, as much as Jesus' conversation with the Samaritan woman had to do with only her, it also had to do with a whole lot more. She is the picture of a people. Her relationship history tells the story of the wanderings of a nation's heart—a nation that was supposed to be wed to God alone but instead went from "husband" to husband.

There is much more to that big picture, and though it's a fascinating study, I'll leave it to the scholars to share. But suffice it to say, if you're like me and you've read the story of the Samaritan woman and thought, *This is not the Jesus I know,* be at rest. As rude as Jesus might have appeared that day, there was no rudeness at all.

Jesus loved this Samaritan woman, pure and simple. He sat there, waiting specifically for her. He sat waiting in the afternoon heat. He would have waited well into the night and then some if he'd had to.

It was his deep, abiding hope that she would come and listen and hear his heart—*his heart for her.* It was his prayed-for longing that she would understand his heart and know his heart for her. Indeed, it was his greatest desire that newness would overtake her own heart and she would walk free of what was obviously a lifetime of hurt unto the salvation of her precious woman's soul.

She was a woman from the village of Sychar in the region of Samaria (see John 4:5). She was a woman despised by the Jews and, because of her history, probably by most of her neighbors as well. She was a woman whose salvation was the man who sat waiting that day—this man who loved her with all of his heart.

JESUS.

You'd have to go a long way, even in our relatively permissive age, to find a woman who's had five husbands—and another man too. It's a bit of a head turner, really. I'm sure even the most "live and let live" among us would raise an eyebrow, or at least chuckle a bit.

I remember once dating a woman who'd had two husbands. She was wise enough to tell me only about the one up front and then wait until I knew her better before she told me about the other. She was so nice and I continued to see her, but I'd be lying if I said it didn't get me scratching my head a little.

Then when I got to know her even better, she told me there was actually a third. She was only thirty-four years old. As you can guess, that bit of news *really* got me scratching my head. Forgive me for being a little indelicate, but as nice as she was, there was something about that information that whispered the word *risk*. I mean, 0 for 3?

Now I obviously told that story a bit tongue-in-cheek; nevertheless, there's a point to be made. We look at a woman who has lived like the Samaritan woman, and even the most understanding of us thinks, *Hmmm*. We ask ourselves, *Who can live like that?*

What's going on with a woman who goes from husband to husband and on and on?

But maybe the better question to ask—*maybe the "Jesus question" to ask*—is what does going from husband to husband and on and on do to a woman's heart?

JESUS.

Once upon a time, there was a Samaritan day for this precious woman that was very different from that day at the well when she met Jesus. It was her wedding day—her first wedding day. Oh what a day that must have been . . .

She had fallen in love with the man to whom her parents had matched her. Following the awkwardness of their first meeting—the meeting that they would eventually laugh together about and tell all their friends about—the love that grew between them was truly a miracle of God's hand. So many of her girlfriends are unhappy, servants to husbands they don't even like. So many of them have come to her privately and cried, "I don't know what love feels like."

But these things are not true of her. She fell *deeply* in love and couldn't wait for her wedding day to come. Now, as she stands by his side beneath the canopy, just moments from giving him all of her heart and all of her everything, she can hardly breathe with anticipation. As she stands mere seconds from putting her life entirely in her bridegroom's hands, she's never imagined a girl could be so giddy with excitement. She's a woman in love, and she's never been more ready or sure.

Then comes the moment when the vow is taken. He looks in her eyes and says, "Till death do us part," or whatever the first-century equivalent would have been. Tears swell in her eyes—she knew they would come. She's longed to hear him speak those words, and they wrap themselves so warmly around her. Like a velvet anchor, they fall from his lips and settle in the deepest, most delicate corners of her heart.

As she looks into his eyes, there is no cause to doubt him. In his eyes she sees the most wonderful man a girl could ever see. Privately, in her heart, she thanks God. She is confident that this moment is born of his perfect will and ordination. And so she hands over her life. She answers, "Till death do us part." The emotion rises so quickly she can barely voice the words. She's just so happy and so much in love.

JESUS.

Late that night she lay with him in the quiet. Oh most wondrous night; he was so gentle and gracious and sensitive. He was not like the husbands in some of the stories she's heard other women tell. Now, here he lies, sleeping at her side where he's promised to lie forever. She memorizes his face by the light of the moon. She memorizes every moment of their day together and every tenderness that was their very first night.

Finally, her eyes get heavy and then heavier. Though she

struggles to keep them open and keep every moment alive, softly they close unto the dreams of sleep. They close unto dreams of the days to come and the children they'll have together, of the home they'll build and the life they'll always live—together.

They close unto all the promises and expectedness that fill any bride's dreams, and unto the hopes that fill every bride's heart.

Then, once upon a heartbreaking time, there came a very different kind of day. It was the day he threw her out. He walked in the door and handed her a certificate of divorce instead of an armful of flowers as he'd done so often when they were first married.

She looked into those same eyes that once said, "Till death do us part," but this time they said something different. This time they said, "I don't want you anymore. You're on your own. I want you out."

They may even have said, "I found someone else," or "She's younger and prettier," and "You're not good enough anymore." We don't know exactly what was said that day or what causes lay at the root of it all. We only know that it must have been awful.

Oh how it cuts to hear such words and to no longer be wanted. How it cuts to have put your life in someone's hands only to have it thrown back at you, to have given your everything only to be told, "I no longer want *you*." Oh how it cuts the most "woman" places of a precious woman's heart.

Dear God, have mercy.

JESUS.

Two thousand years ago, this Samaritan woman was of a rejected race, as the Samaritans were scorned by the Jews who surrounded them. She was of a rejected gender, as first-century women were relatively disregarded and left out. And now, suddenly, her most wonderful wedding day and all the wonder of its promises were torn from her hands. Her wedding-night dreams were crushed to mere fantasies. She stood rejected by the one she loved, and she was suddenly and terribly alone.

What man would possibly want her now? How could she survive without income? And what about her children? How could she ever go back into that house to see them? How could she risk the pain of looking into his eyes again—those eyes that had told her so many wonderful lies but now only push her away and discard her?

But miracle of miracles, another man does come along. She praises God for the answer to prayer and trusts her heart to this man also. He says all the right things and makes all the same vows. He promises to keep and love her forever. He does everything her first husband did—he even throws her out.

Then another man throws her out. And another. And then another man throws her out too.

Finally a man comes along who laughs when she says, "I'll

only do it if you marry me." He laughs in her face because of where she's been in her life, and as broken down as this precious woman has become, she begins to laugh right along with him.

She laughs at the pie-in-the-sky dreams she'd had that first night and at all the wonder that had been in her heart. She laughs at how she'd believed the promises she saw in so many men's eyes. She laughs, thinking, *At least this guy is straight and honest,* and *What does it matter at this stage of the game?* She laughs and laughs . . . and then just gives in.

Rejection is such a terrible thing. It wields the most vicious of blades that strike a woman's heart. Its blade is long and goes in deep. Rejection is a horrible, awful thing.

At its cruel and unforgiving hand, this Samaritan woman was one of the most injured who has ever been. She had suffered so much—five times she'd suffered—and then had done what she had to do to survive. She had been shoved out of innocence and thrust into desperation. Her heart, once soft and alive, now lay crippled, repeatedly pierced and beaten.

Oh Father, how we need you. For any woman who understands the heart of this Samaritan woman all too well, we cry for your mercy, Father!

JESUS.

The woman said, "I know that Messiah (called Christ) is coming. When he comes, he will explain everything to us." Then Jesus declared, "I who speak to you am he."

—*John 4:25–26*

I imagine the moment this woman first came into Jesus' view that sweltering afternoon. He'd been waiting for her for so long. I imagine that sweat was pouring down his face and dripping from his nose. I see his robes soaked many times through. Still he waited, and all the while, under his breath he prayed. *He prayed for her.*

Suddenly he hears the clanging of water jars one against the other. He hears huffing and puffing and a woman's voice swearing at the sun and cursing life. Her angry spewing that flows in the train of so much betrayal grows louder and louder as she climbs the hill toward him.

She steps into view, and his eyes behold what he's known all along in the divinity of his heart. He sees a woman, broken and on guard. He sees a woman afraid and pretending to be strong. He sees a woman so hurt inside and being brave and trying to appear "together."

He also sees that in spite of all the failure and pain, her heart is yearning. Beneath the edge and anger, she privately aches for someone to simply accept her. She cries in her heart, *Won't someone please want me? Won't somebody just take me in his arms and hold me? Won't someone please, please love me?*

JESUS.

Where you and I tend to see only the things on the outside—the sin and bawdiness and the loud, cynical laughter—*Jesus sees a woman's heart.* He hears her cries and counts her tears. He knows her every moment of life and every terrible point of rejection. He knows all the words that have cut her so deeply. Through his Spirit, he was with this precious woman in her wedding-night dreams, and through his Spirit, he wept when they were stolen from her forever.

It was never his plan that her husband would tell her to get out. It was never his desire that she suffer such harm. It was never his hope that she be scared and desperate. Pain was never his promise for her life.

So with all of her woundedness lying open before his heart, his eyes mist over as she draws near. When she sees him, she stops, surprised. She thinks, *What's this guy doing here?* She thinks, *Men . . .* She shakes her head and turns away.

If she'd looked a little more closely, she would have seen his tears. She would have seen they weren't beads of sweat, as she'd assumed at first glance. She would have seen in his eyes and known in her heart, *This man is here to turn my ashes into beauty* (see Isaiah 61:3). *He's here to answer the years of my cries.*

"Will you give me a drink?" Jesus asks. Translation: *I know your thirst, precious woman.*

"If you knew the gift of God and who it is that asks you for a drink, you would have asked him and he would have given you living water." I AM *he who comes to satisfy your thirst. I* AM *to wash your pain away.*

"Go, call your husband and come back." *I have seen your suffering, and I know your pain.*

"The fact is, you have had five husbands, and the man you now have is not your husband." *Oh precious, precious woman, you have seen so much pain.*

Yes, Jesus loved the Samaritan woman. He had not come to condemn her that day. He was not there to hang her sin before her eyes and beat her into repentance with her shortcomings and failures.

He was there to love her—and love her. He was there to wipe every tear from her eyes. He had come to restore her heart after so much suffering and hold her in his arms of eternal salvation.

If I may turn a corner, I know that when Jesus said to the Samaritan woman in John 4:26, "I who speak to you am he," he was saying, "I AM God. I AM Messiah." There are no two ways about that. That is the interpretation clear and away.

At the same time, I have to consider that Jesus spoke those words to a woman who'd been hurtfully handled by many men. She was a woman who longed for a "true" man—one who meant what he said, who did as he promised, and whose promise was forever. A man who would truly give his life for her and love her no matter what, just as a true husband is supposed to do.

This Samaritan woman had been through many men in search of those qualities and securities in love—*and Jesus knew that.* Her longing was ever before his divine understanding as she stood that day in front of his physical eyes. Jesus knew her heart's cry as he spoke those words—just as he knows your heart's cry, oh precious woman, today.

So I just have to wonder something that I'm sure may raise an eyebrow or two, but it just seems so "Jesus," if you will, that I can't resist. I wonder if beneath that declaration of Messiahship, Jesus intended a tiny double entendre. I wonder if there wasn't a tiny undertone that would have spoken into her hunger of heart and would certainly have been truth . . .

I who speak to you am he, precious woman. I AM the one you've been looking for in every way. I AM the only one who can perfectly satisfy the yearning that beats within your heart—the longing to be loved and secured.

I who speak to you am he. I AM come, and I have waited for you. And now that I've found you, I will never leave you. My love for you has been from before the beginning. I promise to surround you all the days of your life, and the banner in which I warp your heart is love.

"Till death do us part," my precious one, and since death for you will now never be, we will never, ever part. So go

ahead and dream your dreams. Let them burn in your heart
with freshness of flame, and giggle away with all the delight
they are meant to bring.

I who speak to you am he, *my precious one.*
I love you. I love you.

JESUS.

[The Lord has anointed me to]
provide for those who grieve in Zion—
to bestow on them a crown of beauty
instead of ashes,
the oil of gladness instead of mourning,
and a garment of praise
instead of a spirit of despair.
They will be called oaks of righteousness,
a planting of the LORD
for the display of his splendor.
                                    —Isaiah 61:3

I love you.
JESUS.

In the sixth month,
God sent the angel Gabriel to Nazareth,
a town in Galilee, to a virgin pledged to be married to a
man named Joseph, a descendant of David.
The virgin's name was Mary.

—Luke 1:26–27

"Behold Your Son"

*S*he was the first "mere human" to feel his presence—literally—as he kicked his little feet from inside her womb. She was the first to hear his words, which were always the Word. Indeed, she was undoubtedly the one who taught him his first word.

She was there when he took his very first steps, and she baked the cake for his very first birthday. She saw him off that very first time he skipped off to school, and she held him in her arms when he came home with a tummy ache.

She was the one who picked him up the first time he fell. He hit his head hard, and she got so scared. He cried and cried; it seemed he cried more than other babies she'd known. It wasn't that he was being a crybaby and it didn't seem that he was in mortal trouble. It was as if he felt the pain more deeply than others, and although he was a mere infant, the look in his eyes was something so different—even haunting—that she kept it to herself, never saying a thing. His look didn't say, "Mommy, do something to take it all away." It was more like, "Such things were never meant to be."

JESUS.

Imagine nursing the Son of the living God. Imagine changing his dirty little diaper and cleaning his messy face after meals.

Imagine watching him play with friends and making him go to bed earlier than he wants to. Imagine standing over his crib and praying over his future. Imagine washing his clothes and cleaning his scraped elbows. Imagine him sitting at the kitchen table, sipping a glass of milk and telling you what he'd learned at school that day.

Then one morning he sits across from you at that same kitchen table, and you can see he's all grown up. You can see in his eyes that he has to go away. He doesn't need to say a word. The look on his face says it all. *I don't know when I'll see you again, Ma. I love you so much.*

You pack him a satchel, and he leaves. And from then on, most of the time you can only watch him from a distance. But when you get the chance, you watch him from close up. Always a mother, you wonder if he's eating right and if people are treating him with care. At the same time, his life has become more than any mother could dream for her son. And so you cheer him onward.

Sometimes you get the chance to sit at his feet and hear his wisdom for yourself. You look around, and you see the crowds. You see lame people walking and dead people breathing. You see thousands who had nothing now enjoying a feast. As you watch and listen, you can't believe he's your child. You think of all those times when you held him to your chest and rocked his tired little boy's body to sleep.

And then one day he hangs from a tree. You watch as they nail your son to a piece of wood. You stand weeping as his blood drips to the ground. Your very own son hangs bleeding from a tree.

Of such was the most privileged woman who ever walked the planet. Of such was a mother named Mary.

Then Simeon blessed them and said to Mary, his mother,
"This child is destined to cause the falling
and rising of many in Israel,
and to be a sign that will be spoken against,
so that the thoughts of many hearts will be revealed.
And a sword will pierce your own soul too."
—Luke 2:34–35

JESUS.

Who was "the virgin Mary"? Who was she *really*? I know she is greatly regarded and revered pretty much across the world. In some circles, she is even prayed to and sung to—even worshipped by some.

I would never seek to take aim at anyone's image of the mother of Jesus. In that role of all roles, she certainly deserves the most tremendous respect. At the same time, truth be told, she wasn't deity. In fact, I can guess that if she could speak today, the first thing she would say is, "Please don't bow or pray to me. I was only a person, like you're a person. Today in heaven I am one of the saints, no different from any other saint—no different from you who have embraced my son as your Savior." Glory to Jesus!

Two thousand years ago, Mary was a woman, pure and simple. She was born of human flesh, just like you and me. I don't mean to ruffle feathers, but we must never forget Romans 3:23 when considering *any* woman or man who is not the living God: "For all have sinned and fall short of the glory of God." In fullness of respect, that word "all" means Mary too. In her own magnificat words: "My soul glorifies the Lord and my spirit rejoices in God my Savior" (Luke 1:46–47), Mary says she needs a Savior just like you and me.

Was Mary a special woman? She was certainly special in the sense that she was chosen among all women in history to bring God's Son into the world and to nurture him unto the release of his purposes. At the same time, that word *chosen* has nothing to do with being greater than anyone else when God is the one doing the choosing. His ways are very different from ours (see Isaiah 55:8), and a quick reading from 1 Corinthians may give us a hint of what *chosen* truly looks like:

God chose the foolish things of the world
to shame the wise; God chose the weak things
of the world to shame the strong.
1 Corinthians 1:27

God sets it up this way so that only he gets the glory. He sets it up so that no one can say, "Wow, look how great that person is!" I would submit to you that in the context of God's choosing anyone to accomplish his purposes—including most precious mother Mary—*chosen* means only *chosen to serve*.

Still, Mary most certainly had wonderful qualities. One need only look at how Joseph respected her when he discovered she was pregnant, not disgracing her publicly as he had every right to do. Look at the way she quietly "pondered in her heart" (Luke 2:19, 51) what she didn't understand, where another would confront, question, and demand. She was obviously a woman who guarded her tongue and walked in godly humility. And, undoubtedly, the greatest evidence of her qualities as a woman is the fact that God knew he could trust her with his Son.

A wife of noble character who can find?
She is worth far more than rubies. . . .
She is clothed with strength and dignity;
she can laugh at the days to come.
She speaks with wisdom,
and faithful instruction is on her tongue.
She watches over the affairs of her household
and does not eat the bread of idleness.
—*Proverbs 31:10, 25–27*

JESUS.

Then there is that one *very* special quality of Mary. It's a quality that puts her in a rare and elite class of both women and men all throughout human history, and in God's eyes it is the one stellar characteristic that sets anyone apart. From the view of his throne room, it is the one attribute that makes any of us truly greater or special.

If I may, I believe it is a quality you have as well—a quality you share with Mary. I can say this with confidence simply because of all the things a woman could be doing with her time today—you've chosen to read this book.

This book is written for a singular purpose: that you might know Jesus a little better, and that you might draw closer to him as a woman and understand his specific heart for you. *Wanting more of Jesus in your life* is the only reason you would pick up this book and read it. If that weren't your passion, you wouldn't have bothered. You would have picked up a novel or a how-to book. You would have purchased a ticket for the latest hit movie.

That quality? *Mary was a seeker of God.* She was a deep and true seeker of God. She was not one to simply shout hallelujahs and "do church." She wanted *him,* and she wanted *more* of him. She desired him fully in her heart. She wanted all of him she could get and did whatever it took to open those doors.

Mary loved and sought after God—and that made her very, very special.

So, who was the virgin Mary, *really*? I just know in my heart that Jesus smiles and nods when I answer in this way . . .

Mary, oh precious and most special woman, was *you*. She was precious, just as you are precious. She was special, as you are special. She even made mistakes.

Most precious and special one—who sometimes makes mistakes—*Mary was a woman like you.*

The LORD looks down from heaven
on the sons of men
to see if there are any who understand,
any who seek God.
—Psalms 14:2

And Mary said:
"My soul glorifies in the Lord
and my spirit rejoices in God my Savior,
for he has been mindful
of the humble state of his servant.
From now on all generations will call me blessed,
for the Mighty One has done great things for me—
holy is his name."
—Luke 1:46–49

JESUS.

The child grew and became strong; he was filled
with wisdom, and the grace of God was upon him.
—*Luke 2:40*

It's no mystery that many more years of Jesus' life are omitted from the Gospels than are recorded. I would guess that a good twenty-five, or even thirty years, are missing. There is a lot of conjecture as to what Jesus did during that time. There are even legends of his traveling throughout the ancient world and stories of miracles. Of course, those are nothing more than folklore.

We know that according to Jewish tradition, Jesus would have studied the Torah as a very young boy. He would have memorized it too. Then there is what I spoke of in earlier chapters—how his father disappeared from the Gospels when Jesus was twelve; most scholars believe he must have died.

Assuming that's true, what would that mean for Jesus, a first-born son in a first-century world? What would that mean for his mother? What would that mean for a woman to suddenly be without a husband to provide and to be surrounded by children to feed? What would that mean for Jesus, whose mother suddenly needed him, literally, for family survival?

I wasn't there two thousand years ago, and of course no one

knows for sure, but I would imagine that it meant life changed radically. I would imagine that Jesus had to go to work. And I would imagine that however old he was at the time—twelve, thirteen, fourteen—little Jesus took his mother under his arm and quickly became a little man.

I think of the day Jesus stood next to his mother as they rolled the stone over his father's grave. My own father passed on just a few months ago, so I know what that's like. Then again, Jesus was probably just a boy when his father died, so I guess I have no idea what that's like at all.

For a boy his age, I have to imagine the depth of loss would be so great that there are no words to describe it. It's like, as they roll the stone over your dad, they may as well roll it over you.

I can also guess that in Jesus's case, the loss went far deeper than just a boy losing his father. I have to believe that Jesus and Joseph spent countless hours doing everyday things and then sometimes doing nothing—together. I picture little Jesus following Dad pretty much everywhere he went. And more than anything else, I see Jesus hanging out with his dad at work, and all the while his dad teaching him his work.

Sometimes Jesus would go with his father to meet with customers and help him carry the tables and doors and other things Dad made for them. I picture little Jesus watching Joseph barter with them over prices and then accept so many "denarii," learning from his dad how business worked.

I picture them together all through the day, laughing and joking and having serious talks too. And I can't help but wonder if, along with the skills of the carpenter trade, Jesus learned integrity from his father—maybe even mercy and faithfulness. Maybe he learned how to treat a woman with care and respect by watching the way his dad was with his mother. Who knows? Maybe it was Joseph who taught Jesus about gentleness, understanding, compassion, and kindness.

No, Jesus and Joseph weren't only father and son. They were teacher and student, mentor and disciple, role model and impressionable young boy.

But more than anything, they were pals. Yes, I have to believe that Jesus and his dad were friends. Good, *good* friends.

JESUS.

Now Dad lies where he'll never be seen again, and Mom can't stop crying. His little brothers and sisters can't stop crying either, just as the tears stream down his own face as well. Through the blackness of it all, however, he calls to memory the time Dad spoke with him about this very thing. As Jesus stands at the grave, holding his mother's hand, feeling it shake and tremble with a deep anguish, he recalls his father's words through the flood of his tears . . .

"If anything happens, son—" Jesus didn't want to hear it and jumped from his seat, but Dad made him sit back down and listen. "I'll need you to take care of your mother. It's the most important thing, Jesus. She'll need you. Your brothers and sisters will need you too. You'll have to be the strong one. It will all be up to you.

"If anything happens, you wipe away your tears and march right into my workshop. [You] pick up the tools I've taught you to use. Go to the villagers and tell them you're the man now. Assure them you have your father's same skills.

"It won't be easy, son, but I want you to look after your mother just as I have. She'll need your protection and your care. She'll need you to provide.

"I love your mommy, Jesus. She's all the world to me. So no matter what, you make sure you take care of her, okay? Do it for me."

JESUS.

So that very day, even as the gravestone settles into its place, young Jesus makes resolve. Not even tomorrow will be lost. As horrible and hard as it's going to be to walk into that workshop without his father, he will do as his father asked. He'll do it no matter how much it hurts and no matter how many tears might fall. He'll do it no matter the cost.

In silent thought, he whispers to the stone as if to his father, "Besides, Dad, I love Mom too. No boy could ever want more in a mother, and I wouldn't let her suffer for even a moment.

"So don't you worry, Dad. I'll care for Mom just as you asked and just as I promised. She'll always know gentleness, security, and care. After all, my father taught me well—and my Father taught me well, too.

"I'll miss you, Dad. I miss you so much already. But don't worry. I'll take good care of Mom. I'll take care of her for me and for you."

JESUS.

No, no one knows what Jesus actually did between the years of twelve and thirty; but if I may, I think he took care of his mother. I think he pushed aside all of his own interests and desires and rolled up his sleeves and went to work. I think he stepped into his father's shoes to provide, protect, and care for her.

Mary had been slammed by life in a broken world—a world in which not even the most "blessed among women" is exempt from its brokenness. There was that long-ago day when little Jesus had fallen and cried, and she'd held him for the longest time, never letting go. Now her tears were flowing, and there was no way—in heaven or on earth—that Jesus would leave her to face this alone.

Here he was, the Son of the living God, and of all the important things he was to be about in the world, he was about taking care of his mother. He would never forsake her. To do so would be a contradiction not only of his human character but of "the Word became flesh" that he so awesomely was.

As the Son of God, Jesus loved his mother as God so loves a woman; and as the son of Mary, he loved her like no son ever did.

He loved her. He loved her.

JESUS.

Near the cross of Jesus stood his mother,
his mother's sister, Mary the wife of Clopas,
and Mary Magdalene. When Jesus saw his mother there,
and the disciple whom he loved standing nearby,
he said to his mother, "Dear woman, here is your son,"
and to the disciple, "Here is your mother."
From that time on, this disciple took her into his home.
—John 19:25–27

It was the darkest of history's days, as Jesus hung limp and bleeding in the afternoon sun. God's plan for our salvation notwithstanding, there was nothing "glorious" about it. They were slaughtering the most wonderful man—the most gracious and humble, giving and caring, faithful and true, compassionate and gentle . . . most breathtaking man there ever was.

This is how the world rewards goodness and love. This is what they do to those who refuse to play their games and who instead stand boldly in the face of wrong. And so there Jesus hangs.

One cannot imagine the horror. We've seen it portrayed in paintings and on screen. There are songs and sermons and books and even painstaking medical analyses. But if I may, even with all that combined together, none of us has the slightest idea.

That day was horror beyond describable. It was horror, period. It was horror at its purest; it was the perfection of horror. Horror alive and horror unchained—and horror at the throat of Jesus.

In the midst of it all, Jesus pushes up his head as best he can and looks out over the hill. He forces open a swollen eye and strains to see. He looks left and right and searches the crowd, and then finally . . . *Mom.*

He knew she would be here. She would never have left him to go through this alone. He can see she's in terrible pain. He can see her tears even through the blood that fills his own eyes and muddies his vision. There were many times when he'd sat her down and told her this day was coming and explained that it would all be okay. But still she cries as her heart rips and tears in love for her son.

Jesus watches his mother from the cross. He watches his mother watch him die. He would love to climb down and wipe her tears away and make her smile all over again. But this is his Father's plan, and he has to walk it through. Still, to see her in such anguish pierces his heart. Even in his own torment, his mother's pain feels like the greatest torment of all.

That's when he remembers . . . *If anything happens, she'll need you.* His thoughts return to that long-ago day when his dad sat him down, and then to that day when Dad was no more. Even as Jesus hangs there, he recalls the promise he made as he held his mother's hand and watched the stone roll over his father's grave. *Don't worry, Dad. I'll take good care of Mom. She'll always know security and care. Besides, I love Mom too.*

JESUS.

In that moment, he thinks back on all the years of sawing wood and hammering nails to make sure she had food on the table. He thinks back on all the times when the two of them sat to-gether at the end of a long day and laughed and talked as mother and son. He remembers the times when he was only a child and she'd held him in her arms until he stopped crying. She never once forsook him. Even unto this day.

With what little strength he still has, Jesus motions with his head for his friend John to bring Mary closer. As they approach, he looks into his mother's eyes, and though his face muscles are too torn to show it, in his heart he smiles.

Then, just as he did for so many years, he keeps the promise he'd made by his father's grave. He does exactly what he'd always done—exactly who he always is. Even on a day like this most terrible day, he pushes his everything aside to take care of his mother.

"Dear woman, here is your son," he whispers through the swelling and pain. "Here is your mother."

JESUS.

I have no way of knowing if what I'm about to write is true. Still, simply based on who Jesus was, I wonder if there wasn't more he wanted to say to his mother in that moment. I wonder if it wasn't just that he was so near death and had so little strength remain-ing, and he just wasn't physically able to voice fully the love that undoubtedly filled his heart.

I wonder if he wanted so much to say to his mother . . .

I love you, Mom. I've never not loved you. Even through the big-ness of all that's happened in the past few years and all the pressure and victory and fighting and crowds, you never once left my heart. While some sons can't wait to leave home and kiss their mothers good-bye, it was always my blessing to be with you. I was always so honored to call you my mother and proud to stand by your side.

I am so thankful for you, Mom. I'm thankful for who you are and how you kept doing for me and smiling and caring, even when you didn't understand. You were asked to serve my Father in the most costly way, and you never complained or questioned. You just gave of yourself and kept giving yourself away.

I am so thankful for the years we spent together, me work-ing in Dad's shop and you being such a blessing. You kept tell-ing me, "Go live your life. I'll be okay." But what you didn't understand is that caring for you was my joy. I would have cared for you even if I hadn't promised Dad. I loved those days and those times, Mom. I wouldn't trade even one of them.

And now it's time for me to go away—although I'll be back very soon. I AM your son, and I AM my Father's Son too, and that only means there is much more to come. It means that all these tears will be no more, and you and I will never not be together—even unto eternity.

So rest, Mom. Rest in your heart. You've done so well, and

you are so precious, oh precious woman—my precious Mom.
I love you, Mom. I love you.
JESUS.

I lift up my eyes to the hills—where does my help come
from? My help comes from the LORD,
the Maker of heaven and earth.
—Psalm 121:1–2

The LORD watches over you—
the LORD is your shade at your right hand;
the sun will not harm you by day,
nor the moon by night.
The LORD will keep you from all harm—
he will watch over your life;
the LORD will watch over your coming and going
both now and forevermore.
—Psalm 121:5–8

Blessed is she who has believed that
what the Lord has said to her will be accomplished!
—Luke 1:45

I love you.
JESUS.

Now one of the Pharisees invited Jesus to have dinner with him, so he went to the Pharisee's house and reclined at the table. When a woman who had lived a sinful life in that town learned that Jesus was eating at the Pharisee's house, she brought an alabaster jar of perfume, and as she stood behind him at his feet weeping, she began to wet his feet with her tears. Then she wiped them with her hair, kissed them and poured perfume on them.

—Luke 7:36–38

"For She Loved Much"

For me, there is no story in all the gospels more breathtaking than this precious woman's story—save the cross and resurrection. There is no gospel personality who more challenges me in my Christian life—no man or woman who more confronts me with how short I fall of the mark and how far I have to go. Even as a man, there is no one I aspire to be like more than this remarkable woman.

I feel this so strongly that if anyone asked me who I thought the greatest role model in all the Bible is, I wouldn't name David, Paul, or any of the supposed greats, as great as they undoubtedly were. *I would name this woman.* For what she did that day and what she must have understood about Jesus comprise the highest degree of human potential and fulfillment of purpose any of us can hope to attain.

Her actions exhibit the pinnacle of Christian maturity. They tell us that in her heart and understanding, this woman was where we're all supposed to be—and where Jesus so passionately draws us toward being, through his Word and Spirit.

There was no "religion" in this woman. There was no scriptural knowledge as we would think of it, no spiritual sophistication. There was just a deep understanding of who Jesus was and is—and there was the *only* response possible when consumed with such awareness.

This woman abandoned herself *completely*. She exhibited no reserve, poise, cool, or caution. She withheld absolutely *nothing*. She threw *everything* on the floor before him.

Brushing all familiarity with the story aside, think of what she did in its raw, nonreligious reality: *She kissed his feet. She wiped them with her hair*. In front of everyone, this woman bent her face to the floor and kissed a man's feet and wiped them dry with her hair.

She gave herself over to Jesus to a degree and in a dynamic that most of us only dream of, entirely overcome in awe and love unto complete "crucifixion" of self.

Oh wonder of wonders in totality of worship!

JESUS.

As I consider what this most breathtaking woman did that long-ago day, it strikes me that there is special significance to a woman's hair. Inspired by the Holy Spirit, the apostle Paul calls a woman's hair her glory and covering (see 1 Corinthians 11:15). On the other side of the coin, when Jezebel sought to entice King Jehu, she painted her eyes and "arranged her hair" (2 Kings 9:30). Sadly for Jezebel, it was the last arrangement she ever made.

There is also a very odd detail in the book of Numbers, as God gives Moses instruction in how to test a woman's faithfulness to her husband.

After the priest has had the woman stand before the LORD, he shall loosen her hair *and place in her hands the reminder offering, the grain offering for jealousy, while he himself holds the bitter water that brings a curse.*
—Numbers 5:18

Why would God specify that a woman loosen her hair when she stands before him in that way? What would that have to do with anything? Not being a scholar, I don't know for sure. Still, there's something about it—a woman loosening her hair—that speaks of vulnerability and abandon and might give us a clue.

The cliché "let your hair down" comes to mind. It means in the name of fun throw caution to the wind. It means forsake reserve and discard discretion.

I think of the classic country song, "Help Me Make It through the Night." The lyrics say, "Take the ribbon from your hair; shake it loose and let it fall." The song speaks of a woman giving herself over to a man. It speaks of her lowering her guard and letting herself go entirely.

And we've all seen the classic movie scene where a woman stares long into a man's eyes. For seemingly forever, she smiles through her stare, and then ever-so-slowly, she lets down her hair. As the screen (hopefully) fades to black, you and I and everyone else watching knows exactly what her falling hair means. *It means she's decided to give herself away.*

All Bible reference aside, it seems that even in the "real world," there's something about a woman's hair. There's something about a woman's taking her hair down and letting it fall. It's a gesture and a sign that signals a decision, a choice. It's an iconic move, if you will, that says, "I give you me. I make myself yours. *I hand myself over—to you.*

And so, as dinner is being served in the home of a Pharisee named Simon, in a room that's filled with the who's who of religious society, a woman quietly kneels at Jesus' feet. The smell of perfume permeates the room, and an alabaster jar lies empty at her side, just as the floor beneath her is stained with her tears. She has just massaged his feet with precious oil and washed them clean with her crying. She has just kissed them— and kissed them.

Slowly she reaches for the pin that holds her hair bound. Everyone freezes just as Jesus holds back his own emotion in silence. She slides the pin free, and her hair cascades to the floor. She bows before Jesus, draping her tresses over his feet, and saying without words, "I give you me. I make myself yours. I hand myself over. You are my Lord."

Jesus said to her, "Your sins are forgiven."
The other guests began to say among themselves,
"Who is this who even forgives sins?"
Jesus said to the woman,
"Your faith has saved you; go in peace."
—Luke 7:48–50

JESUS.

One of the most glaring realities of Jesus' life is something I've never heard preached or discussed, although I'm surely not the first to recognize it. Forgive me if I ruffle some male feathers, but it is an undeniable and unarguable reality—not to mention downright embarrassing to those of us who are men.

As recorded in the Gospels, when push came to shove, it was the women who truly "got it" with regard to Jesus. It was women who showed Jesus deep and complete faithfulness and love—just like this woman who so remarkably humbled herself before him. Women were the ones who cast themselves wholly aside in worship and affection. They were the people who walked with Jesus in devotion and commitment to the end, even unto personal risk.

Throughout the pages of Matthew, Mark, Luke, and John, wherever you see someone *extremely and entirely* abandon themselves unto Jesus in heart, mind, spirit, and soul—it's a woman.

Yes, there were men who called him Lord and men who bowed down before him. Yes, it was a man who proclaimed, "You are the Christ, the Son of the living God" (Matthew 16:16). But at the end of the day *where were those men?*

Among the disciples—supposed friends and followers of Jesus—with the exception of the apostle John, only women stood with Jesus at the cross (see John 19:25 and Matthew 27:55–56). The men left him to hang on his own. And the man who'd proclaimed that Jesus was the Christ was busy denying he ever knew Jesus and cowering somewhere in mortal fear (see Matthew 26:75).

It was men who challenged Jesus every step of his way and a man who betrayed him. Men were the ones who lied and cheated and plotted behind his back to kill him. It was "us guys" who ran away with our tails tucked between our legs and left Jesus alone when he needed us most. It was men who doubted, argued, insulted, and rebuked him—and men who spit in his face.

On the other hand, it was woman who cared for Jesus' needs all along the way (see Luke 8:3). It was women who wept for him on the Via Dolorosa (see Luke 23:27) and who followed him to the cross and went to the tomb to prepare his body (see Mark 16:1).

It was a woman who anointed him in the days approaching the crucifixion (see Matthew 26:7), a woman who wouldn't leave his tomb and couldn't stop crying before it (see John 20:11). Among the mighty apostles we know and love, it was a woman who ran with the news that Jesus was risen (see John 20:18)—a woman who immediately believed it.

And it was a woman who bowed her face to the floor before him. It was this most precious woman who loved him so deeply that she actually kissed his feet.

Did you know it's the only kiss Jesus is recorded to have ever received? Oh I'm sure there were many more, but it is the only kiss the Holy Spirit of the living God immortalized and made alive in the living Word—other than Judas's.

JESUS.

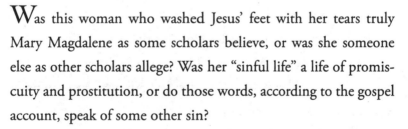

Was this woman who washed Jesus' feet with her tears truly Mary Magdalene as some scholars believe, or was she someone else as other scholars allege? Was her "sinful life" a life of promiscuity and prostitution, or do those words, according to the gospel account, speak of some other sin?

Who knows, and even more, what does it matter? She was a sinner just as we all are. She was a sinner who most breathtakingly found Jesus!

I picture the room, that Galilean day, packed elbow to elbow with the town's most esteemed and self-important citizens. Jesus was in attendance, and there can be no doubt that the entire community was abuzz. Everyone would have wanted to see the man whom the whole ancient world was talking about. They would have heard all the rumors of great miracles and would have relished the chance of actually seeing one.

Then of course there was the possibility that sparks would start flying, which is always exciting entertainment. Everyone knew that the Pharisees were trying to discredit and destroy Jesus—and here he was dining in a Pharisee's home. If I may phrase it nonreligiously, a ringside seat at that dinner table would have been the hottest ticket in town.

I can see all the guests decked out in their finest and most fashionable clothes. I picture each of them vying for the cushion seats closest to Jesus. That's not because they were seeking or believed him, although I'm sure every crowd had some who were sincere. It wasn't necessarily that they hungered for righteousness or wanted to get their lives in order.

Rather, they wanted to be close to the action. They didn't want to miss out on the latest. This party was the go-to event of the year—dinner with Jesus—and everybody who was anybody would have made sure he was there.

There's also a certain upscale sense to this dinner, although we have no way of knowing for sure. Generally speaking, the Pharisees were businessmen who were committed to the Law and the Prophets. They were merchants and such, and they were highly respected and admired throughout society. One would guess that this Pharisee named Simon would have gone all-out to impress his honored (yeah, right) guest. I would imagine he brought out his finest "china" and hired extra servants. I see him slaughtering his fattest cow and ordering the fanciest cakes for desert, sparing no expense to put on a good show.

And that's exactly what it was—a show. Simon's efforts were not so much to bless anyone, but rather to hold advantage. Simon knew that Jesus lived a minimalist lifestyle, and by hanging affluence in his face, Simon makes the statement, "I'm better than you." He says to everyone there, "This guy's a nobody." It's an old businessman's trick. You get them in your home court and intimidate them with your wealth, and then you smile as you proceed to "cut their throats."

I could be wrong, but I'm guessing that was the atmosphere in Simon's home that evening. There's Simon sitting in the seat of honor, a full-bellied man, full of himself and surrounded by those who would lick his boots. There's Simon relishing the prospect of stumping Jesus in front of them all.

I picture the room packed and hot, steaming with the smells of too much rich, spicy food. I picture eager and wanting faces all around the table, lining the walls, leaning in the doors and windows, all on the edge of their seats hoping to see some "action."

And I picture Jesus sitting quietly in the middle of it all. He knows every hostile thought and ulterior motive that ricochets off the walls and presses in upon him. He knows that he sits as a lamb among wolves. Yet deep inside, Jesus smiles. He smiles for what he knows is about to happen. He smiles because of who he knows is just outside the door.

JESUS.

***

One wonders how this woman gained entry into the party that evening. As it seems she wasn't a stranger to anyone, she couldn't have slipped in unnoticed. She obviously had a reputation in town, and a bad one at that. People knew her, and for whatever reason, they knew every unseemly detail about her.

When the Pharisee who had invited him saw this, he said to himself, "If this man were a prophet, he would know who is touching him and what kind of woman she is—that she is a sinner."
—Luke 7:39

I can only guess she was a woman for whom the saying stands true, "where there's a will, there's a way." And therein was the key—it is the most golden of golden keys—*overwhelming passion to get to Jesus.*

I picture her pleading with the servants who stood guard at the door. I even see her going to her knees and begging them to let her in. After all, who cared if they laughed and called her a fool? She had nothing to gain by being proud and everything to lose if she were kept from Jesus. Can you imagine all that was burning in her heart to make her so passionately driven?

Perhaps there was a day, long before, when she was going about her sinful life and saw a crowd massed in the market. Men were jeering and shouting insults, and she wandered over to see what was happening. Or maybe it wasn't mockery that caught her attention at all. Maybe she was passing along and suddenly heard a man's voice cry from a depth of soul she'd never before imagined, "I'm gentle and humble in heart! *Come to me!*"

Being a woman who was obviously maligned, she would have stood in the shadows and stayed in the back. I imagine her rising on her toes to see over the heads of the many people. Suddenly the man standing in front of her takes his wife by the arm and grumbles, "This guy's mad." He pulls his wife and child away, and that's when she sees him for the very first time—Jesus.

I don't know what she may have heard Jesus say that day.

"I am the way and the truth and the life."

"The kingdom of heaven is like treasure hidden in a field."

"Your Father in heaven is not willing that any of these little ones should be lost."

"Let the little children come to me."

I don't know what she may have heard—but I do know what she saw. She saw a man who was the Son of the living God. She saw a man who was compassion and care incarnate. She saw a man who did not hold her faults before her and who offered her love and all the salvation that goes with it.

And as a result, her life would never be the same. It was as if her heart was opened up and she could feel again. The callus that had grown thick around it and so ugly and hard was melted away. All the terrible things that had meant so much to her and had become her life over the years—it was as if they were gone. They were washed away and removed with one breath-stealing look from his eyes.

Now, here Jesus was having dinner at Simon the Pharisee's house in the nice part of town. Here was this man who had dramatically changed her life, and he doesn't even know about it. She'd never had the chance to say thank you that day. Overcome with emotion, she ran home and then cried all night and woke the next morning an entirely different woman. She dressed and hurried back to the marketplace, but everyone said Jesus had already gone.

Now he's returned. Her savior is so near! And so she presses through the crowd toward Jesus. Some of the guests step back when they see her face. They look with disgust and whisper, "Who let her in here?" She sees the looks and hears the whispers, but they mean nothing to her. They can say what they want—what matter such things? She just pushes on and presses through. She weaves left and right and crawls over this and wiggles past that, making her way toward Jesus.

And then suddenly she's there! He's reclining on the cushion just before her. She stands trying to catch her breath as the whole room turns to stare. She swipes the perspiration that's about to fall from her nose. She brushes the hair away from her face and straightens her robe over her shoulder.

Jesus lifts his eyes. He smiles. He reaches his hand and smiles even more—*and that's when the tears begin to flow.*

She wasn't intending to cry, but there's just no stopping it. It feels as if everything inside of her is pouring out and there are no words, but only tears. She tries to say she's sorry, that she can't help herself, but it's impossible to speak. She can only weep before him.

Jesus is everything to this precious woman—his love caresses her heart, and her wounds suddenly don't matter anymore. She instantly feels life again, and feels it abundantly. In a moment, her everything is nothing but loss, compared to him.

This Jesus who is reaching his hand to her and smiling with so much affection in his eyes—this man whose feet are now soaked in her unplanned tears—could only be God, and this woman knows it. Oh how deeply this precious woman knows it. And oh, how life-changingly right she is!

JESUS.

There is only one possible response when a person is standing in the presence of the living God and fully absorbs all that that means. He is Adonai. He is El Shaddai. He is the Everlasting One, the Most High God. That response is to come unglued and fall on your face before him.

We see it with Daniel, Ezekiel, and everyone who stood eye to eye with God in ancient times. That's why I say this woman understood what very few embraced in the company of Jesus two thousand years ago, although it hung so obviously before everyone's eyes. I'm sure there were others—I hope there were others—but she's *the only person on record* who reacted as the ancients did.

And so she goes to her face and kisses his feet. It doesn't matter that her face scrapes against the floor. Oh such precious freedom from self to love Jesus as she did! What a gift. What a goal for us all to aspire to.

She kisses his feet and doesn't stop kissing them. She tastes her own tears that have washed them so clean. She tastes the dust and sand that once soiled them. She kisses and weeps and kisses and weeps.

Then comes the moment when she raises her hands to take down her hair. I imagine you could hear a feather drop in that room, as if it wasn't already piercingly silent. Here were all these people trying so hard to be impressive—and here was this most amazing woman.

She's worried that she's made a mess. She only wanted to thank him, and she's cried all over his feet. How like a woman to think such a thing, and so she reaches for the pin that holds her hair from falling to its length. All through her life people have told her she had beautiful hair, and she has always been so thankful for it. Her hair is her "glory," her "covering"—her woman's crown of beauty.

But all that means nothing when it comes to Jesus. Crowns are only meant to be laid before him. So slowly she slides the pin free. Simon and his guests can barely breathe. Her crown cascades to the floor in a luscious mane that would fill any woman's heart with envy. It falls and falls as she lowers her face and lays her curls upon his feet.

JESUS.

[Jesus] turned toward the woman and said to Simon, "Do you see this woman? I came into your house. You did not give me any water for my feet, but she wet my feet with her tears and wiped them with her hair. You did not give me a kiss, but this woman, from the time I entered, has not stopped kissing my feet. You did not put oil on my head, but she has poured perfume on my feet. Therefore, I tell you, her many sins have been forgiven—for she loved much. *But he who has been forgiven little loves little."*

—Luke 7:44–47

As I read those words, I can't help but wonder what Jesus did shortly after he spoke them. I can't help but wonder if he rose from the dinner table and thanked Simon for the extravagant meal, as he signaled to his apostles that it was time to leave. Perhaps he took this precious woman's arm in his and moved "the party" to her house in the not-so-nice part of town.

I can't help but wonder if they all spent the remainder of the evening sitting under the moon outside her cottage, laughing and talking and sharing the wonders of his kingdom that was yet to fully come.

This woman had blessed Jesus so much. She had given him the honor he was due. She was one of the few who really *knew* who he truly was. Even among the apostles who surrounded them that night, she was one of the very few.

Yes, I imagine Jesus and this woman sitting and laughing side by side, perhaps on a little bench or around a fire. I imagine them sipping first-century tea from "china" that was far from the finest. I can guess she asked him questions about this and that, and he happily answered every one.

I imagine that the love for Jesus she felt in her heart only grew with each passing hour, long into the night. And I imagine that the kingdom love she saw beating in his heart, through the windows of his eyes, was so overwhelming at times that she had to turn her own eyes away.

She was a woman who loved Jesus very much—and whom Jesus loved even more. And so, through the warmth of his presence and manner that night, he most surely whispered into her heart just as he whispers into your heart by his Spirit today . . .

I have seen and felt your love, most precious one, and you have no idea what your love does to me. I am "weak" with your love as it pours like oil over my heart. I rise from my throne in explosive joy as it washes over me like a shower of tears. I roar in

*majesty as it blankets my being like a swath of luscious beauty.
I am taken to silence as it kisses every corner of my kingship.*

*Yes, my precious one, I am taken by your love—and I so
love you, too. I long for that eternal day when I can literally
wrap my arms about you and you will live hidden in my
embrace*—forever.

*This is what I "live for," my precious one. This is what
I died for.*

I love you, precious one. I love you.

JESUS.

*The twenty-four elders fall down before him
who sits on the throne, and worship him who lives for ever
and ever. They lay their crowns before the throne and say:
"You are worthy, our Lord and God,
to receive glory and honor and power,
for you created all things,
and by your will they were created
and have their being."*
—Revelation 4:10–11

I love you.
JESUS.

As Jesus and his disciples were on their way,
he came to a village where a woman named Martha
opened her home to him.

—Luke 10:38

"Martha, Martha . . ."

As sad as it is, religious art and gospel movies have always treated our precious Martha somewhat poorly. I've never once seen her cast or painted as beautiful—always quite the opposite. They never dress her in attractive colors but always in grays and earthen browns. In fact she's usually portrayed wearing a first-century apron.

And did I mention that she's always older? She had a sister named Mary who is forever portrayed as younger and prettier, although there is nothing in Scripture to indicate that was so. Mary is the sister who is dressed in blues and bright colors in films and paintings—and probably in most of our imaginations as well.

As Martha's story goes, Jesus and his apostles dropped in for dinner one day. Martha began rushing about, preparing the meal and I'm sure a whole lot more. All the while, her sister did nothing. She sat listening to Jesus—as Martha probably would have loved to do herself. But as it worked out, Jesus told Martha that Mary's way was "better."

> *"Martha, Martha," the Lord answered, "you are worried and upset about many things, but only one thing is needed. Mary has chosen what is better, and it will not be taken away from her."*
> —Luke 10:41–42

As a result of those words, Martha has forever been banished in our collective thinking to second place. She "lives" evermore in her sister's shadow. Mary is the one we adore and aspire to be like. She's the forever example of right posture before the Lord.

Well, I hope you don't mind if I throw in my two cents. Forgive me for speaking what is purely my own feeling. I appreciate Mary, and as Jesus said that day, surely listening at his feet was the better way. Still I much prefer Martha. Oh please give me Martha! She so obviously lived to make Jesus happy. Between her and sister Mary, Martha was the one who thought not of herself but dug in her heels and rolled up her sleeves and went out of her way—*for Jesus.*

Let's have some fun and do a little role-playing, putting ourselves in "Martha" shoes. Imagine that it's a typical, busy—if not frenzied—afternoon. In this day and age, no matter what our lifestyles may be, we all seem to have plates that are over-filled. So I'm guessing this scenario isn't too much of a stretch for anyone.

Perhaps you're working hard at your job, trying to meet deadlines and resolve crises. Maybe you're rushing from meeting to meeting. Or maybe it's one of those days when your coworkers aren't pulling their weight, the boss is on edge, and nothing seems to go right.

On the other hand, you may be a full-time mom. That would make your afternoon even more hectic. Being a mom is undoubtedly the most demanding occupation on the planet.

You might be a student or a grandma—there are many possible scenarios and all kinds of settings that fill every woman's life with activity. Besides, no one is allowed to sit on the sidelines in our little drama. So think about your own particular busyness, and the stage is set.

Let's say your phone rings. You reach to answer, but *Unknown Number* shows up on your caller ID. You hesitate, thinking it may be a telemarketer, and that's the last thing you need in the middle of all that is going on. Still, it's better to be safe than sorry, so you decide to answer it anyway. "Hello?"

This is where our role-play gets difficult. Now you have to really use your imagination . . .

You say hello, and the voice that greets you in return belongs to the Son of the living God. It is Jesus on the line—the Creator of the universe, El Shaddai, Adonai, Mighty God Jehovah—in human reality and existence.

The voice you hear is the physical manifestation of the very same voice that spoke your life into being—*and you know it.* It is Immanuel, God with us. It is the King of kings and Lord of lords breathing and alive, and he's calling to speak to you. Can you even begin to imagine?

JESUS.

He says that he, his twelve buddies, and a handful of others are coming to your town, and he was wondering if they could come by. He tells you that the journey has been long and hard and the preaching has been even harder. Jesus asks if you could possibly put them up for the night, "if it isn't any bother."

You being who you are, the first thing that races through your mind is that the refrigerator is empty and they must be hungry. After kicking yourself for putting off the grocery shopping, you ask Jesus if they've had anything to eat. For a moment he hesitates, but as we all know, he is one who doesn't lie (I couldn't resist that), so he tells you the honest truth, "No, but we'll run to the store and pick something up. Don't trouble yourself about it."

Of course you'll hear nothing of the kind, so you tell Jesus that you'll take care of everything. You tell him to come over immediately and that they can stay as long as they want, and you ask if there's anything else you can do for him. He says no and thanks you for being so kind. Then you hang up the phone and probably fall on your face overwhelmed in awe and trembling.

After all, Jesus is coming to your house. Jesus is coming to dinner. Jesus is coming to stay—*with you*. Again, can you imagine anything more mind blowing or breath stealing?

JESUS.

Now here is where you begin to tell the story. *What happens next?* You know that Jesus is making his way over and he'll be knocking on your door in, let's say, two hours. Where does your mind immediately go? What's the first thing you do?

Before you answer, may I say that you have to play fair. There's no being "religious," if you know what I mean. You are confronted with the very practical reality that Jesus himself is coming over, and there are a whole lot of people coming with him. In the middle of what is already a busy day with a packed schedule, what would you now do?

I know everyone is different, and every woman is unique, but if I may suggest, tongue-in-cheek, my guess is that you'd panic. You'd look at your watch and start listing everything in your head and realize it's nearly impossible to do everything that needs to be done. Then you'd quickly shake your panic off, as women are so wondrously gifted in doing; you'd roll up your sleeves and begin to attack that list with all that you are.

They will need to be fed. They need beds to sleep in. They could all probably use a hot shower, and their clothes will have to be washed and maybe even mended.

My guess is that you'd kick yourself a second time because the house hasn't been cleaned in much too long, and the breakfast dishes are still in the sink. Your mind would go to all the home repairs you've been putting off and the mismatched towels hanging in the bathroom and the kitchen rug that you should have replaced a long time ago.

You would want everything to be absolutely perfect for Jesus. He's not only God, who obviously deserves the best, but he's done so much for you, and you'd want to honor him in every way. It's not merely a matter of hospitality or making your guests comfortable—it's a matter of giving your best to your Savior.

So there will be no throwing hamburgers on the grill. That would undoubtedly make Jesus happy, but for you it most certainly won't do. After all, is that what you'd feed Billy Graham or whoever else you may highly esteem? How much more does the Son of the living God deserve! What could you possibly prepare for him that would make you feel like you'd done him justice?

Still you have to prepare something, so you roll your sleeves up even more and go all out in every way. You run to the best market and ask the butcher for his finest cuts of meat. You grab the freshest vegetables, and then it's off to the bakery for their freshly baked bread. You race home, whip out your most special recipes, and cook up the grandest meal you've ever served.

Then you rush about and tidy the house. You pull out your best of everything, putting brand-new sheets on the beds and hanging your fanciest towels in the bathrooms. You put fresh flowers on every table, and on and on.

Your sole desire is to make Jesus happy. All you want is to please and honor and bless him, to thank him with everything that you are, for it's because of him that you are who you are. He has so deeply touched your life—and now here is your chance to somehow touch his in return.

So it doesn't matter how busy the day is—you will find a way. No expense will be spared, and no effort is too much. You put your head down and you "do" like you've never done before. It's all for Jesus, and so you get busy and *do*.

Again, casting all religious posture aside, I have to guess that most every woman reading this page would say, "Yes, that's probably how I would respond. I would definitely want to show Jesus as much care and tribute as I could. I would be so overwhelmed that he would come to my house, and I'm so thankful for what he's done in me, that I would do everything possible to bless him." Amen!

Well, obviously Martha's phone didn't ring that day two thousand years ago. My guess is that Jesus, being sensitivity and graciousness in the flesh, sent word ahead of his arrival as best he could. We have no way of knowing those details, but I think I can say with confidence that however Jesus' visit unfolded, Martha probably reacted to it . . . well . . . a lot like you would.

Yes, our precious Martha was probably—and may I also say *hopefully*—a woman much like you.

JESUS.

What was that day like for Martha two thousand years ago? Life was just as busy back then as it is today, except in a first-century sort of way. So just as you were in our little role-play, I have to guess that Martha, too, had been working long and hard.

Perhaps she had children to care for—maybe she had many of them. The gospel account doesn't mention Martha having a husband at the time—it's even implied that she didn't. That would mean Martha had to provide for herself and her possible children along with whatever other demands confronted her. One can only imagine the pressure that kind of lifestyle would impose on a woman living in Martha's era.

Then suddenly her house fills with wall-to-wall visitors. It wasn't only Jesus and his troupe of disciples who came to her home that day. Word would have spread quickly throughout Martha's village of Bethany, and virtually everyone would have wanted to come over. News also would have spread to the villages beyond, and many of those folks would have come to see Jesus too.

Based on her words to Jesus—"My sister has left me to do the work *by myself*" (Luke 10:40)—I'm going to guess that Martha didn't have servants or any helpers. It's remarkable that no one offered her a hand. You would think someone would notice and say, "Martha, is there anything I can do?" instead of what she was probably hearing: "Martha, can you bring us some more figs?" *Most especially from her own sister.*

Forgive me, but I don't condemn Martha for speaking up like

she did. I know that I would have said something too—not that that makes it right, of course. But here was Martha giving and giving, and everyone around her was sitting and *taking*. She was trying so hard to bless Jesus and accommodate her company and was probably entirely exhausted.

Martha was distracted by all the preparations that had to be made. She came to [Jesus] and asked, "Lord, don't you care that my sister has left me to do the work by myself? Tell her to help me!"
—*Luke 10:40*

Profoundly, I just have to believe that Martha wanted to sit at Jesus' feet too. *Oh how we miss that Martha also loved Jesus.* She undoubtedly wanted to drink of his leadership and care, right along with Mary and everyone else who was crowding her home.

But there was too much work that had to be done, and no one else was doing it. The word "distracted" gives that away. It means that Martha was trying, but there was too much else that stole her attention.

And we must never forget that Martha was the one who ran to meet Jesus when he came to Bethany after her brother, Lazarus, died. She ran to meet him alone—while her sister didn't make a move.

When Martha heard that Jesus was coming, she went out to meet him, but Mary stayed at home.
—*John 11:20*

Yes, Martha dearly wanted to sit and listen to Jesus along with everyone else that day. I believe she desired that with all her heart. She wanted to know Jesus more deeply and completely. She wanted to taste of his righteousness and enjoy the beauty of his mercies and have her heart filled to its fullest with his love.

She longed to sit at his feet and drink of his ways and bathe herself in every second of Jesus' most precious presence, just like her sister, Mary.

JESUS.

But Martha had a little "problem" with sitting at Jesus' feet that day. Her problem was a testimony to the quality of her character and was intimately intertwined with the excellence that was Martha: *his needs were more important than hers.*

If she did what she truly wanted to do and sat down by Jesus, who would dress his bed and make sure his dinner didn't burn? Who would wash his trail-weary robes and keep his bathwater from getting cold?

She could see the dark circles beneath his eyes, and she could hear the scratch of tiredness in his voice. Martha was the kind of woman who couldn't ignore such things and had to do something about them. I wonder if she thought, *Why don't they ever let Jesus rest?*

So Martha stepped up to the plate. She took it upon herself to make everything right. Where no one else was willing, she made an active choice to deprive herself of what she surely wanted most, and she got busy—*serving.*

Forgive me for speaking so boldly, but I honor that choice.

Jesus' words notwithstanding, someone has to stand up and do the work. I praise God for a woman who rolls up her sleeves while others sit "in the pews." Praise God for a woman who pushes personal want aside—a woman who rises above her own needs and gets down to the business of actively loving and serving others.

[Jesus] told them, "The harvest is plentiful, but the workers are few. Ask the Lord of the harvest, therefore, to send out workers into his harvest field."
—*Luke 10:2*

Then I heard the voice of the Lord saying, "Whom shall I send? And who will go for us?" And I said, "Here am I. Send me!"
—*Isaiah 6:8*

Praise God for Martha and for all of you Marthas who follow in her ways! Glory to Jesus!

If I may, I'd like to interject a short personal story. It's about my ministry administrator and assistant. Her name is Sharon—but we could easily call her *Martha II* . . .

I do a significant amount of ministry in South Africa, and so Sharon and I travel to that country three or four times every year. We serve thousands during each visit through evangelistic outreaches, feeding, clothing, skills training, and so on. Of all my ministry work, this South African involvement is hands-down the most exciting and satisfying.

Sharon's focus is ministry to the "kiddies," as we have come to call the children. She goes into the schools and into the streets and trains church leaders in children's ministry techniques. Every night she conducts a Kiddies Crusade, where the children gather to hear the gospel of Jesus and enjoy good food and have a ball. Hundreds of South African children come to the Kiddies Crusade each night, and you can only imagine how they fall all over "Sister Sharon," as she is so affectionately known to them.

Walking through the villages and townships with Sharon, all you hear are children's voices calling, "Sister Sharon! Sister Sharon!" They cry out from every township nook and cranny, and of course they all come running to hug and play with her. Sharon has truly done a wondrous work among these precious South African kiddies, and they absolutely love and adore her.

JESUS.

During our most recent trip, I woke one morning at the house where we were staying and walked out of my room to find Sister Sharon standing at a table on the porch before a literal mountain of bread. I couldn't believe my eyes. I'd never seen so much bread in one place in my life. And there stood Sharon before it all, with a butter knife in her hand and two five-gallon buckets of peanut butter. She was making hundreds of sandwiches for the kiddies who were expected to come to the service that evening—many of whom would not have eaten otherwise.

Sharon would stand there, spreading that peanut butter, literally for hours into the afternoon. She would do the same thing the next day and the next and the day after that and the day after that . . .

JESUS.

Sharon is sixty-three years old as I write these words. She lives by herself in a small town in Indiana. Sharon never married, having lost her fiancé in the Vietnam War. She serves in her church and in a local homeless ministry too. Several years ago she battled colon cancer, and today she's battling rheumatoid arthritis.

There are times in South Africa when the kiddies are climbing all over Sister Sharon, and I look at her face and can see she's in pain. On this last trip, there were days when the hours of standing at that table making all those sandwiches greatly inflamed her condition.

Whenever I see her like that, I tell her to stop, but she looks at me as if to say, "Someone has to do it." I tell her to forget the sandwiches, and she answers, "The kiddies need to eat." I tell her not to let them climb on her like they do—"But they need so much love."

When Sharon returns from a South African trip, she steps off the plane and walks to her car. She pulls out her keys, throws her luggage into the trunk, climbs behind the wheel, and quietly drives home.

Maybe on the way Sharon stops at her favorite coffee spot for a cup of familiar joe—I don't know. But I do know there's no reception awaiting her. I know there's no applause.

For Sharon there's only serving—serving Jesus and his little ones, who are forgotten by so many yet lying deeply in the heart of Jesus. There is only going and doing the work that wins no awards or praise, and then there is going home.

Boy, I love the Marthas of our world. Don't you?

JESUS.

Returning to that Bethany day two thousand years ago, did Jesus really chastise Martha as his words to her seem to do? Oh to be chastised for giving of yourself. Have you ever tried so hard to do what is right and yet somehow it ended up wrong? Have your best intentions and efforts ever backfired in your face?

Did Jesus truly chastise Martha that day—*or does it just appear that he did*?

If I may, I'd like to answer that question with three words taken from the Gospel of John. They are the framework within which Jesus' "Martha, Martha . . ." must be heard if the story is to be accurately envisioned in the deep of our hearts:

Jesus loved Martha *and her sister and Lazarus.*
—*John 11:5*

This may come as a surprise, but of all the people who were around Jesus two thousand years ago, there are only four in all the Gospels who are specifically named as "Jesus loved . . ." One is Mary, one is Lazarus, one is "the disciple whom"—and the other is *Martha.*

No, I can't imagine Jesus hurting Martha with his words in a million, billion years. I can't imagine him embarrassing her in front of everyone, as it would appear that he did. I'm sorry, but it is just too contrary to who Jesus is. It clashes too much with those three little words that pull back the curtain on his heart for Martha and whisper the truth that surely would have saturated every syllable he ever spoke to her.

Jesus loved Martha pure and simple, and out of that truth flowed all his actions toward her. From that singular and breathtaking reality, his every word, tone of voice, action, and glance poured forth from his heart unto hers.

Perhaps the words they exchanged that day were spoken in private. Or maybe Jesus stood and took Martha into his arms and smiled from ear to ear as he said, "Martha, Martha." Perhaps he even had some fun with her in that moment, kissing her on each cheek as he spoke her name with such greatness of affection.

Who knows if beneath his words Jesus was saying, *Martha, I'm okay. It's time for you to sit and rest. You've been racing about and you've done a wonderful job—dinner and everything is great. But now it's time to come sit at my feet, here next to your sister.*

She needs me so much, Martha, and I'm not going to turn her away. Just look at her face and into her eyes and you'll see. You need me too—more than I need what you're working so hard to give me.

So come and sit, most precious Martha, whom I love and appreciate so much. As you have been working hard to serve me, let me now serve you. Come and sit, Martha. Rest at my feet.

JESUS.

No one knows any of those particulars, of course. But surely such tenderness and warm understanding would have been much more consistent with who Jesus was than exalting one sister at the other's expense. Jesus' heart was flooded with nothing less than the fullness of his affection for this woman named Martha. After all, she was a worker and a giver . . . *kind of like him.*

Who is greater, the one who is at the table or the one who serves? Is it not the one who is at the table? But I am among you as one who serves.
—*Luke 22:27*

The greatest among you will be your servant.
—*Matthew 23:11*

In closing, I can't help but wonder about something that makes me chuckle a tiny bit. Mary sat transfixed on Jesus to the exclusion of all the work that her sister, Martha, was doing. Mary's intent was to drink of Jesus' everything and learn all that she could from him. Even her sister's obvious need for a helping hand wasn't going to get in Mary's way.

Well, I wonder if Jesus' "message" that day was on giving. I wonder if he spoke of sacrifice and how his Father's kingdom is built on the hearts of those who selflessly give themselves away.

I wonder if Mary heard Jesus talk of the beauty of servanthood and the preciousness of a woman whose heart was set on pleasing him, while most others wanted him to please them. I wonder if Jesus spoke of how deeply a child of his who thought and lived in that way touched his heart.

If Mary didn't hear that kind of message that day, then she surely would have heard it from Jesus some other time. You see, Jesus loved Mary's sister, Martha—and he loved Martha's ways.

He loves you, precious "Martha," and he loves your ways.

He loves you.

JESUS . . .

It is true, my precious one who desires so much to please me. I have seen your work and the way you serve. I have seen how you do the work no one wants to do, and even though you get tired sometimes, you never complain. You just give and give yourself away.

I know about the time you drove home, crying all the way. Oh how you felt so unappreciated and wondered what it was all for. I know about the time you watched that other one get so much attention for doing so little, and you felt passed by. Still you got back up and continued to give.

It's woven into the fabric of who you are, and it makes you so lovely a woman. When everyone else has gone home to their own, it's you who stays and finishes. You're the one who commits and comes through. You never waver and nothing is ever too much. I love you for that, my precious one. You are so lovely to me. You are my delight.

As a man two thousand years ago I, too, was one who rolled up my sleeves. It was never my way to do nothing while others worked or to say I was too tired or that some task was beneath me. Yes, my precious one, when I walked in your world, I was a worker too—just like you.

Do they call you a Martha and chuckle a little as they say the words? Do you often think that of yourself? Never forget my Word, oh precious woman, where it says, "Jesus loved Martha." And never, ever forget—Jesus loves you too.

I love you, my precious one. I love you.

JESUS.

*O Lord, God of Israel, there is no God like
you in heaven above or on earth below—
you who keep your covenant of love with your
servants who continue wholeheartedly in your way.*
—*1 Kings 8:23*

*For your love is ever before me, and I walk continually in
your truth.*
—*Psalm 26:3*

His banner over me is love.
—*Song of Songs 2:4*

I love you.
JESUS.

As the Father has loved me, so have I loved you.

Now remain in my love.

—John 15:9

"Remain in My Love"

*T*hey were some of the last words Jesus spoke before he was arrested and marched to the cross—"Remain in my love." I was not there, of course, but I can only imagine that he spoke them with tears of tremendous passion, for Jesus knew they were the key to every hope and salvation he'd come to provide.

Whether it be yesterday, today, or forever . . . *Remain in my love.*

JESUS.

We have had the pleasure of meeting some very precious women in these pages. It's been my honor to share them with you, and I trust that you've grown to experience and know them a little better in your heart than you may have known them already.

We've met eleven women. We've met single women and wives

and mothers and even a little girl. We've met women who were alone and some who were surrounded by others. We've met women who made mistakes and women who suffered at the hands of those they trusted. We've met women who, although their lives were filled with pain, pressed ahead in spite of it all, and we've met women who were terribly buried by pain and walked with no hope at all.

Taking the leap across time, the bridging reality between us and them is that not much has changed in two thousand years. Of course, being a man, there is no way I truly can claim to understand women. But it's my guess that women today are very much the same as women were two thousand years ago—*in their hearts.*

I'm speaking of a woman's hopes and desires and joys and pleasures. I'm talking about the kind of experiences that are shared by women of all cultures and all times. The dreams-come-true events that fill a woman's heart and make her giddy with excitement, the experiences that a woman "lives for," counting the days till they arrive. Womanly confidence and peace fill her heart when she stands on the safe and secure ground of expectations met and dreams fulfilled.

Then there are those things that shake a woman's world and make being a woman so very hard. Instead of healing, they bring harm; instead of protection, they conjure fear. A woman suffers loss today just as she did two thousand years ago. Broken trust and betrayal run rampant. There are unforeseen illnesses and errors in judgment, sin and the shame that follows in its trail. A year often turns into decades, and so many dreams never come true.

And in the midst of all the good and not so good, there is that most remarkable and specifically female hope that keeps a woman's chin forever held high. She meets the day no matter what is thrown at her and fixes her eyes on the next horizon. In spite of all that confronts her or doesn't work out, as long as there are tomorrows to come, promise lives in her heart.

JESUS.

I'm guessing that you may have seen a little bit of yourself somewhere in the lives of the women we met. You may have identified with the joys and strengths and graciousness of some of them. Perhaps you saw yourself in their giving and commitment and their pressing through and pressing on. You may have recognized their ethic and desire to serve. Or maybe in your own heart, you know the depth of their love for Jesus and the excitement of their little-girl dreams.

On the other hand, it may be their hardships that strike a familiar chord. We've explored many hurtful scenarios, and tragically, today's world is just as broken as the one in which those precious women walked. As much as humanity has advanced in two thousand years, a contemporary woman's life is subject to many of the same heartrending realities faced by the women of Jesus' day.

Like some of those first-century women, perhaps you, too, have been through divorce or lost a husband or child. Maybe there were mornings when you woke to a man who was not your husband. Perhaps your history—like that of several of the women we've met—is filled with sorrow. Maybe you feel burdened to the point of being bent to the floor, or you've made so many mistakes that you wonder if it even matters anymore.

Then again, you may just feel exhausted and alone, your womanly hope nearly worn down.

> *Hear my cry for mercy*
> *as I call to you for help,*
> *as I lift up my hands*
> *toward your Most Holy Place.*
> *—Psalm 28:2*

JESUS.

In reply to every one of those possibilities, may I quote my (retired) pastor, Jack Hayford: "We live in a broken world full of broken people who cut each other with the jagged edges of their broken choices and ways." And may I add that none of us is exempt. Oh Father, have mercy.

I mention this to remind you that Jesus was never the author of any woman's pain. We grossly misrepresent him when we paint the picture of an angry God, sitting on his throne slinging lightning bolts at people. Or even worse, intentionally meting out tragedy to carve out purpose.

Some may argue with me on this, but I ache in my spirit when I hear that cliché talk, "God is putting you through trials, sister. He's doing a greater work. Count it all joy!"

Forgive me for getting on a soapbox, but I'm not convinced that's the way it works. Again, *we live in a broken world.* It's not God who pulls triggers—it's people. It's not God who causes accidents or walks out the door and leaves a wife or plants cancer in a body.

This crippled, imperfect creation is what plants cancer in a body. And it's a world where everyone (including you and me) is broken and filled with a sin nature that throws so many lightning bolts at a woman's life.

Where does the purpose come in? Jesus takes those terrible things that happen to us all and miraculously brings good out of them. It's called redemption, and he is ever redeeming. Saving and turning things around is his full-time occupation, twenty-four seven. He is *forever* taking our ashes—whether we created them ourselves or they were thrust upon us—and turning them into beauty (see Isaiah 61:3).

We know that in all things
God works for the good of those who love him,
who have been called according to his purpose.
—*Romans 8:28*

If I may, Jesus only loves—pure and simple. He never does not love. He only loves and never does not love—*you*.

His thoughts toward you are pure and holy. Passion for you consumes his heart. All his ways are strong and gentle. All his ways are faithful and caring.

Jesus never turns his back and never once leaves you, even though it sometimes feels as if he has. His eye is always on and ever for you.

And oh how he smiles. He smiles because he loves you. Indeed, you are his delight.

JESUS.

Whichever of these women you've identified with and in whatever ways you've understood them, an even higher hope lies in the pages of this book: that somehow, a little deeper and maybe more intimately, you've freshly discovered *him.*

Back in the first chapter, we began with *a man's heart is revealed in his actions.* In every one of these women's lives we saw Jesus act in faithfulness and strength on their behalf. We watched as he handled them with kindness and tenderness. His purity of intention and protectiveness toward them have taken our breath away. Over and over, we saw him stop what he was doing and go *so* out of his way.

Jesus healed their wounds with compassion and washed their

souls with truth. He healed their bodies, too, and he raised them from the dead and breathed life back into the hopes of their hearts.

We saw him want *nothing* from these women—and only give of himself to them. We saw Jesus care, and only care.

He met these precious women right where they were, whether that meant in heartache or loss or sin or brokenness. He treasured each and every one of them, no matter how rejected, self-destructive, destitute, or laughed at they may have been. We even saw him wrap his arms around a woman who was filled with demons and escort her into places of honor.

He lifted up these precious women no matter how deeply they were buried or had buried themselves, and he restored their dignity and womanly value. He treasured and respected them and sheltered and served them.

We saw Jesus smile upon every one of these women and smile because of them. He wrapped his arms around their trembling shoulders and cried right along with them. He went to his knees in the sand before them and reached his gentle hand into their hearts. He lifted their countenances and looked into their eyes and wiped away their every tear.

We saw Jesus cherish these women and carry their names into history. We watched him laugh with them and sit and chat and enjoy their company.

In other words, we saw Jesus love them—*and only love them.*

JESUS.

It's certainly no mystery at this point, but that word *love* is the bottom line of every Jesus moment we've explored. It's the essence of who Jesus is and what lives in his heart, just as it's the overwhelming truth of every one of these women's stories from two thousand years ago—and of your story today.

I've written "love" so many times in these pages that I run the risk of your growing tired of it. On the other hand I cannot imagine that a woman would ever tire of Jesus' love. I have to believe that a woman would want to wrap herself in its most breathtaking reality and live every moment of her every day in the safety of its promise.

Have you lost much in your life? *He loves you.* Was your childhood far from the best? *He loves you.*

Did you make more mistakes than you care to recount? Has there been so much hurt in your life that you're not sure you can feel anymore? Or do you dream many dreams and live excited and expectant to see his promises come true?

He loves you.

JESUS.

If I may ask, why don't you say it with me this time—except make it your own? Say it aloud just as he would whisper it into your heart. It's the truth beyond all truth, you know. It's his truth for you.

He loves me.

Jesus loves me.

He loves me with all of his heart.

JESUS . . .

Yes, my precious, I do. And you are ever so lovely in my eyes— you are my treasure and delight.

What is past means nothing, precious woman, and today is a brand-new day. It is your brand-new day. Yes, from this moment on, your future is fully in me, as you rest in my arms of gentleness, truth, compassion, and care.

I see your heart, and your heart makes me smile. I reach into your heart that you might smile even more. I will never abandon you, precious woman. Indeed, I never have.

Oh I know it can be hard to live life in your world sometimes. You must never forget that I walked in it myself. And I also know the specific hardships that can befall a woman such as you.

This I know because I created you. I breathed you into

being because I wanted you. And as I look upon you even now, I want you all the more.

You are altogether lovely, my precious one. I am entirely taken with you. You are my happiness, and you bring me joy.

I know that's not always easy for you to believe, and as long as you walk in your world of brokenness and limitation, you can never know it in fullness. But one day you will fully understand, my child—when you and I are together in my glory. Oh for that day when we're eye to eye and forever together.

I "live" for that day to come, my beloved. On that day the first thing I will do is reach out my hand and wipe away every tear you ever cried. There will be no memory of hurt or things done wrong. There will only be me and you. *The promise of that day is my precious delight. Oh, how I yearn for that day when I will take you in my arms and never, ever let you go.*

As for today, my child, I say blossom. *Leave behind what is behind, and as a woman, stand tall and flourish. Be renewed, healed, and strengthened. Let every promise in your heart be revived and all your hopes made alive again. Live every moment* free!

You're an absolutely beautiful woman, my most breathtaking one. I know that's sometimes hard for you to truly believe, but you must cast illusion aside and see who you really are—in me.

I love you, precious woman. I'm the living God—and I love you.

That's who you are.

I love you; I love you.

JESUS.

The Lord appeared to us in the past, saying: "I have loved you with an everlasting love; I have drawn you with loving-kindness.
—*Jeremiah 31:3*

You are a garden fountain, a well of flowing water streaming down from Lebanon.
—*Song of Songs 4:15*

As the Father has loved me, so have I loved you. Now remain in my love.
—*John 15:9*

I love you.

JESUS.

About the Author

Bruce Marchiano is an actor, author, and international speaker best known for his portrayal of Jesus in the film *The Gospel of Matthew*. Marchiano has penned several books on the life and person of Jesus. Among them are *Jesus Yesterday, Today & Forever; Jesus Wept;* and the bestselling *In the Footsteps of Jesus,* all of which have been honored by the Evangelical Christian Publishers Association as Gold Medallion finalists. Marchiano's book *The Character of a Man* is a character profile of Jesus as the model of manhood and masculinity.

As a popular Christian speaker here in the United States, Europe, Australia, South Africa, New Zealand, and Canada, Marchiano has ministered the love of Jesus in every imaginable setting, from churches, universities, banquets, and conferences to prisons, high schools, and stadiums. Marchiano is also the founder and president of Marchiano Ministries, a nonprofit organization principally involved in South Africa, where Bruce conducts crusades, builds homes for the poor, plants and builds churches, and provides entrepreneurial training/opportunities for young people who have no hope otherwise.

Also available
by Bruce Marchiano

Jesus Wept highlights the love of Jesus and the profound truth that God is near, even in the midst of pain.

In *The Character of a Man*, Bruce Marchiano explores the humanity of Christ and how we can emulate Him.

BRUCE MARCHIANO

JESUS WEPT

1-58229-350-3

THE CHARACTER OF A MAN

Reflecting the Image of Jesus

BRUCE MARCHIANO

1-58229-494-1

HOWARD BOOKS
A DIVISION OF SIMON & SCHUSTER